Once theology and mysticism start to drift apart
the former tends invariably to become a "theology
of concepts," an abstract science, a mere religious
philosophy. Those who teach theology cease to
live up to it as the mystics did. In order to return
to the great age of theology, dogma must be
brought back to life and mystically experienced.

— Sergius Bolshakoff, *Russian Mystics*
(Kalamazoo: Cistercian Publications, 1976), p. xx

# THE WOMAN, THE HOUR, AND THE GARDEN

A Study of Imagery in the Gospel of John

ADDISON HODGES HART

WILLIAM B. EERDMANS PUBLISHING COMPANY
Grand Rapids, Michigan / Cambridge, U.K.

Published 2016 by

WM. B. EERDMANS PUBLISHING CO.

2140 Oak Industrial Drive N.E., Grand Rapids, Michigan 49505 /

P.O. Box 163, Cambridge CB3 9PU U.K.

www.eerdmans.com

Printed in the United States of America

22  21  20  19  18  17  16      7  6  5  4  3  2  1

Library of Congress Cataloging-in-Publication Data

Names: Hart, Addison Hodges, 1956–    author.
Title: The woman, the hour, and the garden :
a study of imagery in the gospel of John / Addison Hodges Hart.
Description: Grand Rapids, Michigan : Eerdmans Publishing Company, 2016.
Identifiers: LCCN 2015046673 | ISBN 9780802873392 (pbk. : alk. paper)
Subjects: LCSH: Women in the Bible. |
Bible. John — Criticism, interpretation, etc.
Classification: LCC BS2615.6.W65 H37 2016 | DDC 226.5/06 — dc23
LC record available at http://lccn.loc.gov/2015046673

Cover art: sculpture of Mary Magdalene by
Lucy Churchill © 2016; www.lucychurchill.com

Unless otherwise noted, the Scripture quotations in this publication
are from the Revised Standard Version of the Bible, copyrighted 1946, 1952
© 1971, 1973 by the Division of Christian Education of the National Council
of Churches of Christ in the U.S.A., and used by permission.

For DBH

# CONTENTS

A Note from the Author about
the Art in This Book    ix

1. Introduction: The True Witness    1

2. Excursus: The "Virgin Mother"
in Christian Typology    27

3. "The Woman" and the Women
Addressed as "Woman" in John    41

4. Excursus: Life and Death in John    55

5. The Woman and the Garden    77

6. Our Present and Future Life    91

# A NOTE FROM THE AUTHOR ABOUT
# THE ART IN THIS BOOK

READERS WILL SURELY notice that, throughout this book, I have used the art of Albrecht Dürer (1471–1528) to "tie together" its six chapters. My reasons for this are twofold — one simple and subjective, and the other slightly more complicated and also subjective.

The first reason is that I have always been fond of Dürer's works. Even as a boy, I found his paintings and engravings alluring, and I could happily spend long periods of time (at least, "long" as children reckon the passage of time) studying the details of this or that image.

The second reason for my choice is that Dürer stands, in the history of Western art, at that point where the Medieval and the Renaissance meet. Dürer was a Christian Humanist in the mode of Erasmus, a lifelong Catholic, an admirer of Luther (notwithstanding his own Catholicism), a progressive thinker in his day, and possessed of (in Giorgio Vasari's words) an "extravagant imagination." In other words, his art drew together the traditional, the intellectual, and the imaginative; he was able to present biblical imagery (as we see in our six selections here) in sometimes startling and unexpected new ways, and yet to imbue them with the rich traditional typology of centuries.

Who better, then, to illustrate a book on the imagery of John's resplendent Gospel? John likewise exhibits an "extravagant imagination," and the Johannine corpus — perhaps the most striking in the whole New Testament for subtleness and refinement — draws together (from its own first-century Judeo-Hellenic-Christian context) the traditional, the intellectual, and the imaginative. So, with that highly subjective reasoning in mind, I *naturally* chose Dürer to set the "mood" for this small book. I think it's a match.

# ONE

# INTRODUCTION: THE TRUE WITNESS

The Ecstasy of Saint Mary Magdalene (c. 1501-1504)

*This is the disciple who is bearing witness to these things,
and who has written these things; and we know that his
testimony is true.*

JOHN 21:24

**T**HIS SHORT BOOK was born partly out of a reaction to
the canard that Jesus was married to Mary Magdalene.
It is an assertion we have heard repeated in recent decades,
and at the time of this writing it is yet again in the news,
and doubtless it will crop up again. I have no interest in
addressing the topic directly, however. I bring it up only to
confess what moved me to write this brief study in the first
place, and to say that the idea that Jesus was (or, rather,
is) "wed" is a metaphor as old as Christianity itself. Where
the sensationalists who claim that Jesus was a married man
make their primary mistake is to misread early Christian
metaphors as being historically suggestive of some long-
buried facts, usually purported to be long buried by a con-
niving, conspiratorial church hierarchy. What it shows is
that *literalism* is not merely a fault of believers; it can also
be detected among those who regard belief as naïve. The
latter can be as deaf and blind to metaphor and symbol as
any literalist believer.

But this book is not a defense of church hierarchy or a refutation of sensationalism. Every year we have some new sensation about Jesus Christ trumpeted by the media, usually around Easter and Christmas. It has almost become an annual holiday tradition, like Easter-egg hunts and stockings "hung by the chimney with care" on Christmas Eve. This is not, though, a book of apologetics; but it is about a "code," and specifically it is about a "code" of imagery and language employed in the New Testament writings attributed to John (the Gospel and three Epistles, omitting Revelation). This is scarcely a new thought about John, even if I am using a term ("code") that was already worn out — again, by those making sensational claims — ten years ago. The Fathers and Medieval Doctors, Eastern and Western, always read John as a "spiritual gospel," meaning that its deepest and most important message required proper unveiling and interpretation within the assembly of believers. We can justly regard it as a coded language addressed to the initiated and baptized.

There are important words that John repeats throughout his writings, and an earnest study of these words provides keys to unlocking crucial themes again and again. I would like, then, to look at how John uses the image of "the Woman" in particular in his Gospel. That will occupy the central place in this book, but it cannot be divorced from other images and phrases that are related by John to this image (e.g., "the hour," "the garden," and many others). "The Woman" is, I believe, a more central "icon" within his overall vision of Christ's significance than might be immediately apparent. I will put forward the suggestion that this image points us towards the Christian community's sacramental identity itself (one might say "herself"). But I do not wish to get ahead of myself at this stage. It is enough to say that I believe that John fully intended for his work to be "spiritually" interpreted, and not read in strictly literal terms of history; that, in fact, the meaning of Christ's appearing among human beings is best expressed through imagery and words carefully chosen, and that he saw this mythopoeic approach as presenting the truest revelation of the gospel. I believe that John's Gospel is a theological work above all else, shaped by real history, but overlaid with an "iconographic" or "sacramental" use of metaphor.

Here I make a caveat. If one means by the term "theology" the rational study or systematic arrangement of religious doctrine, then the author of the fourth Gospel did not write "theology." John was not constructing a system of thought. Nor was he consciously contributing to what is often referred to as "New Testament theology," nor, for that matter, was he consciously contributing to a church-approved collection of books called the New Testament. We do not know what he might have read of other texts later included in the New Testament, or even if he had read any at all. Whatever others were writing in the first century about Jesus, John and his community were writing in a clearly different literary style and presenting a distinctive view of Jesus and his meaning.

If, however, one means by "theology" what the Eastern Christian tradition means by the word *theologia*, then John is the theologian par excellence. *Theologia*, in this latter sense, refers to a mystical intimacy with God, a contemplative vision of truth; it is revelation that can be *indicated*, but not fully explicated. Reason (*logos*) plays its part, but it is God's reason and not man's and must be disclosed. Reason is thus what is being unveiled, not the instrument that does the unveiling. Human reason is insufficient for that. In Eastern Christianity (and the New Testament is entirely *eastern*), theology is not a rationalistic endeavor, but direct knowledge of God and personal relationship with him. It is primarily receptive, not intellectually inventive. In both the Syriac and Greek patristic traditions, theology was poetic and mystical above all. In short, theology is prayer, with the human mind being the receiver of divine input. As one of the greatest desert fathers of the fourth century put it, "If you are a theologian, you will pray truly; and if you pray truly, you will be a theologian."[1] John "the Evangelist" (or, "good news bringer") was a "theologian" in that ancient Eastern sense.

As for "John" himself, we can't be sure that he was, as tradition has it, John the son of Zebedee, the Galilean fisherman and brother of James. He may have been, but he may not have been. Tradition makes that connection, and it's a venerable one. We can say, with good reason, that he is likely the one referred to in the Gospel anonymously as "the disciple whom Jesus loved" (John 13:23; 19:26; 20:2; 21:20), a phrase meaning that he was Jesus' "close friend." Curiously, the only other anonymous person in the Gospel, closely related to Jesus, is "the mother of Jesus." And, like "the beloved disciple," she is never named (John 2:3; 19:25-27).

Others than John have been proposed as the possible author and the anonymous "beloved disciple." For example, Nicodemus, the Pharisee who came to Jesus by night and had a private discussion with him (3:1-15, or 3:1-21), has been suggested. We are told that the beloved disciple was known to the high priest (7:50), and that would have been true of any Pharisee who was a member of the Sanhedrin, as Nicodemus was. And, too, Nicodemus was in Jerusalem

1. Evagrius of Pontus, *Chapters on Prayer*, 60 (cf. Robert E. Sinkewicz, *Evagrius of Pontus: The Greek Ascetic Corpus* [Oxford University Press, 2003], p. 199).

at the time Christ was crucified (19:39-42). This proposal appears plausible; but we still must reckon with the fact that no early tradition identifies Nicodemus with the beloved disciple, and, without more substantial basis, "circumstantial evidence" of this kind is just speculation.

Nor is there a single author of the Gospel. We must accordingly revise any simple notion we may entertain of the book's composition. This detail is indicated by the verse quoted at the beginning of this chapter: "We know that his testimony is true." The "we" in this case refers, it seems, to the Christian community for whom the Gospel was composed, or possibly to those elders of the community who could vouch for the authenticity of the testimony recorded. The Gospel as we have it was almost certainly an edited text, with expansions and alterations, all in an attempt to clarify its message. The "we" in the verse could well be those who had a hand in shaping the final form of the testimony of their founder, presumably the beloved disciple.

It is a conjecture, but a sound one, that the community had formed around this particular disciple of Jesus. He had been their teacher, and an eyewitness to Jesus. He had laid the groundwork for the community's understanding of who Jesus was, and who they were in relation to God through him. He had gathered them into fellowship with himself, and, through him, with Jesus, and, through Jesus, with God. He had been the voice for them of the promised "Paraclete" (meaning "one who stands alongside" in order to strengthen or encourage), who is also named "the Holy Spirit" (meaning "holy breath" or "holy wind"), teaching them "all things" and bringing to their "remembrance" what Jesus had said (John 14:26). In the community's shared imagery of their teacher's role, he had been the one "lying close to the breast of Jesus" (13:23), near (in other words) to the hidden secrets of Jesus' heart, and therefore the one best able to interpret him; just as Christ — "the only Son" — had from the beginning abided "in the bosom of the Father," and was thus uniquely qualified to make the Father "known" (1:18).

The same writer or writers would express the same idea in the First Letter of John this way: "That which we have seen and heard we proclaim also to you, so that you may have fellowship with us; and our fellowship is with the Father and with his Son Jesus Christ" (1 John 1:3). And the great third-century church father, Origen, clearly understood the vital link between Jesus and the beloved disciple and the community of the beloved disciple, when he wrote that Jesus left "to him who lay on Jesus' breast the greatest and most complete discourses about Jesus."[2] The commu-

2. Origen, *Commentary on the Gospel of John*, Bk. 1, Ch. 6 (cf. *Ante-Nicene Fathers*, Vol. 9 [Peabody, MA: Hendrickson Publishers, 1999], p. 300).

nity was privileged to have, in turn, leaned on "the breast" of John, so to speak, and heard his testimony.

So it was that, after his death (the implication of John 21:23), with "the Spirit of truth" still guiding them "into all truth" (14:17; 15:26; 16:13), the community's chief representatives believed they could say with real plausibility, "*We know that his testimony is true*," and, further, they regarded themselves as authorized to flesh out his "memoirs" with expansions, supplements, and, it seems, the final overall shape. ("Memoirs" — *apomnemoneumata* — was a term that second-century Christians such as Justin Martyr used when referring to the Gospels.)

With all that in mind, we come back to the point made at the outset, that the Gospel of John is not a work of theology in any rationalistic sense. It is not a work of linearity and systematic logic. Its doctrines are not encased in hard-and-fast terms; and its images and language are *poetic*. As poetic, the language adopted is also *intentionally ambiguous* at times (this is a vital point, as we shall see). It is *theology* in the mystical and contemplative sense of the word. It is a "testimony," not a doctrinal scheme or part of a greater system called "New Testament theology." It is about "truth" (*aletheia*), which is not *simply* to be understood as biographical accuracy or historical detail. Historical and biographical information are certainly present, providing the framework of the book. But the Gospel of John, in its final shape, is a *poetic work* with a *carefully chosen vocabulary* that holds the key to its deepest meaning. Understand the language, the vocabulary, and "the doors of perception" will be "cleansed."

When it says in the Gospel that the "signs" it records "are written that you may believe that Jesus is the Christ, the Son of God, and that believing you may have life in his name" (20:31), this is not a revivalist invitation to "receive Jesus into your heart" in some emotional way, nor is it a dogmatic definition one is being asked to endorse formally in a merely cerebral manner. It is an invitation to "come and see" (1:39, 46) and *experience* for oneself a transformative way of living in relation to God, and within a community of spiritual participation.

And it is the community's poetic lexicon, the very language and words used and woven like gold threads throughout the tapestry of this Gospel, that renders John's distinct portrait of Jesus. The words that John uses, metaphorical and flexible and ambiguous as they are, are meant to awaken "belief" (not to be confused with either a rush of feelings on the one hand, or an intellectual assent to propositions on the other), which in turn leads to the special kind of "life" Jesus offers. We might say that John's Gospel is "iconographic" in nature. John creates "icons" in language — literary imagery that is not just to be "seen," but *seen through*. In his hands even historical characters and events become representative features in his total picture. We shall, in fact, be exploring this very thing in this book.

John displays remarkable skill for using Greek words effectively, a fact already recognized in the early third century by Origen. He understood John to be a proficient theologian, taking great care with his artful use of language. Notably, John makes the most of metaphors (for example, bread, light, door, shepherd, resurrection, road, vine), and of the multiple meanings contained in a number of Greek words (e.g., *logos* [which can mean "word," "message," and "reason"], *doxa* [which can mean both "glorious radiance" and "praise"], and *ano* [which can mean both "again" and "from above"]). If the latter are not "portmanteau" words of the Lewis Carroll variety, they are at least words that are portmanteaus of meaning — that is to say, each one is a "suitcase" full of various interpretive possibilities. It is probable that John would not have us choose *either* this meaning *or* that meaning with such words, but rather that we should take them and their host of meanings together — a sort of wordplay. So, for instance, *doxa* means *both* glory (radiance) *and* praise. What we can justly call John's work of *literature* suggests to us that, although the author's and editors' first language may have been Aramaic and the frame of their minds Semitic, their choice of *Greek* words was brilliant and utterly unforgettable. In places the Johannine poetic vocabulary conjures up mythological themes from the earliest chapters of the book of Genesis, in other places it is witty in its use of verbal ambiguity, and it always makes rich use of profound and multivalent metaphors. The poetic imagination is coupled in John with an evident facility for Greek vocabulary, and the result is an enduring masterpiece of poetic prose.

The purpose of John's poetic language is always to bring us into a direct encounter with "truth." It does so by offering the reader "mind-blowing" ways of looking at Christ and his significance for the world (one will forgive, I hope, my brief lapse into language derived from the 1960s).

Two quick examples might help. Christians are, of course, accustomed to hearing that "the Word became flesh" in Jesus Christ. Too often, though, we hear it only as a doctrinal proposition that must be affirmed. But, in our familiarity with this statement, we may have lost something of the surprise that this idea originally excited in its hearers. We are inured to the wonder of it through repetition. We barely bat an eye at the downright weirdness of the notion. Early hearers, on the other hand, with sensibilities shaped by centuries of teaching that heaven and earth could not be unified in a material body, felt their whole understanding of life shift, shaken by the unnatural idea that the divine up above, dwelling in refined regions of pure spirit, had joined itself with the lowly, earthy, bodily muck we live in down below. If one took that seeming contradiction into one's thoughts, which is presented right at the very outset of John's Gospel, it opened up an entirely new vision of *reality* — which is what the word "truth" (*aletheia*) essentially means in John. Things could never be the same again after such a realization.

Another example is the way that the word "judgment" (*krisis*) is used in John. The early readers of the work may well have fully expected a coming day of judgment, a final reckoning, when God, or his representative, Christ, would assemble the peoples of the earth and divide the good from the bad (e.g., see Matt. 25:31-46). At that future event there would be a vindication of the righteous and a condemnation of the wicked, and it was firmly scheduled for a day and time known only to God. When the Gospel of John refers to the judgment, it never denies a future judgment, and the community of John certainly believed that there would be one; but at the same time the Gospel insists that the judgment is happening *right here and now*. One provocative statement might even be considered something like the Christian equivalent of a Zen *koan*. Jesus says: "Truly, truly, I say to you, he who hears my word and believes him who sent me has [now] eternal life; *he does not come into judgment, but* has [already] *passed from death to life*" (John 5:24; emphasis mine). (A parallel assertion of Paul's — just as daring — is Romans 8:1: "There is therefore now no condemnation for those who are in Christ Jesus.") This is one of those many proclamations that would have rocked the minds and expectations of those hearing the Gospel for the first time.

Theologians, with their propensity for categorizing these things, have called this "Realized Eschatology," to distinguish it from "Future Eschatology." John's hearers would have been stunned by it, not "theologically informed" by it. They might find themselves, consequently, reevaluating all their hopes and fears in the light of it. They would have been stirred up by the surprising thought that the future had somehow taken place in the here and now; the "future" judgment had already intersected with the world and every human life; infinite accountability was involved in each person's decisions and actions; the "last things" were present things.

The Gospel of John may be the production of a profoundly theological mind, but the author also possessed the qualities of a poet. Jesus is an enigma in John's work, not entirely grasped by such conventional titles as "Christ," "Son of God," "King," and so on. Always, throughout John, there is a push to go beyond such terminology, which is never adequate. Jesus is constantly pushing against glib titles and definitions, forcing his followers to expand their understanding of who he is, to go deeper and further in their belief. He remains cryptic in his challenges, constantly pushing them to grasp ever more of the truth. Whenever they think they have his identity suitably defined, he strains them to take in yet more. Note in the following passages how he moves them beyond their comfort zones and easy definitions, challenging each of their conceptions every step of the way:

Nathanael answered him, "Rabbi, you are the Son of God! You are the King of Israel!" Jesus answered him, "Because I said to you, I saw you under the fig tree, do you believe? You shall see greater things than these." And he said to him, "Truly, truly, I say to you, you will see heaven opened, and the angels of God ascending and descending upon the Son of man." (1:49-51)

Perceiving then that they were about to come and take him by force to make him king, Jesus withdrew again to the mountain by himself. (6:15)

So Jesus said to them, "Truly, truly, I say to you, unless you eat the flesh of the Son of man and drink his blood, you have no life in you; he who eats my flesh and drinks my blood has eternal life, and I will raise him up at the last day. . . . This is the bread which came down from heaven, not such as the fathers ate and died; he who eats this bread will live for ever." This he said in the synagogue, as he taught at Capernaum. Many of his disciples, when they heard it, said, "This is a hard saying; who can listen to it?" But Jesus, knowing in himself that his disciples murmured at it, said to them, "Do you take offense at this? Then what if you were to see the Son of man ascending where he was before? It is the spirit that gives life, the flesh is of no avail; the words that I have spoken to you are spirit and life. But there are some of you that do not believe." For Jesus knew from the first who those were that did not believe, and who it was that would betray him. And he said, "This is why I told you that no one can come to me unless it is granted him by the Father." After this many of his disciples drew back and no longer went about with him. (6:53-54, 58-66)

His disciples said, "Ah, now you are speaking plainly, not in any figure! Now we know that you know all things, and need none to question you; by this we believe that you came from God." Jesus answered them, "Do you now believe?" (16:29-31)

The identity of Jesus is conveyed through an accumulation of poetic metaphors, images that convey an identity that cannot be simply defined or reduced to any conventional title such as "Messiah" or "King." John is leading his readers to interpret Jesus in an ever-deepening, more radical, and more startling way. The closest we come to an unambiguous statement is near the end of the book, when Thomas, encountering the risen Christ, cries out, "My Lord and my God!" (20:28); and, while this is undoubtedly the denouement of the Gospel's message, it is still not a definition that can be taken in any glib sense. The thrust of the entire Gospel cautions us not to allow ourselves to become comfortable with a limited "resolution" to the mystery of Jesus. There is always more to be revealed to us in our union with the Word, and the "code" is always beckoning us to dig in deeper.

Thus the Gospel of John gives us a wide variety of metaphors for Jesus: Word, bridegroom, bread, light, door, shepherd, and so on. If one scans the array of images, one cannot fail to see how greatly they differ from one another in themselves, while, at the same time, they all have *Jesus* as their center and point of reference. Bread, for example, is nothing like light, and a bridegroom is quite a different thing than a door; yet all these images are used to identify Jesus.

Seven metaphorical sayings in particular stand out in the Gospel. Seven times Jesus says, "I am" this or that, and we should not ignore the implication of the phrase "I am" in each instance. It is the divine name given to Moses by God in Exodus 3:14. Beyond doubt, Jesus is divine in John's Gospel; and John knows that divinity itself is not something that can be contained in human terms. We are dealing with that which transcends all human conception. One must approach it in a roundabout way, and John — like all great mystical theologians before and since — does so in poetic language. Jesus says:

"I am the bread of life." (6:35)

"I am the light of the world." (8:12)

"I am the door of the sheep." (10:7)

"I am the good shepherd." (10:14)

"I am the resurrection and the life." (11:25)

"I am the way, and the truth, and the life." (14:6)

"I am the true vine." (15:1)

All these, along with other metaphors (such as "word" and "bridegroom") not among these seven "I am" statements, are images for the person of Jesus and indicate who he is in relation to us (including, I should add, the metaphor of "bread"). In each instance of the seven "I am" statements, Jesus is saying that he is somehow "like" the illustration used.

What John is doing in his Gospel is inviting the community to reflect on what it means for Jesus to be our sustenance ("bread") or our guidance ("light") or our immortal hope ("resurrection"). It is, as we have noted above, an invitation to a realization of Jesus' identity and nearness, to an experience of the enigmatic "I am" at the center of this circle of poetic metaphors, where they are all joined to the person of Jesus as spokes to the hub of a wheel. To change the analogy, each metaphor serves as a way in to an ever-deepening knowledge of Christ. As sources of inspiration and insight, none of them can be fully exhausted.

And if John is a book primarily centered on the identity and meaning of Christ, it is secondarily about the identity of the people gathered together in a union with God through him. As I have already noted, this book is about one image or icon of the church in particular: the figure of "the Woman." The key passage for the discussion is an enigmatic statement of Jesus, which — in the original Greek — is far more interesting than most translations, if not all, render it. With that verse as the launching point, we will look closely at the three women in the Gospel whom Jesus pointedly addresses as "Woman" to ascertain whether or not that address contains more than a literal meaning. It is my argument that it does in each instance, and that the image is an important one — and it may especially be relevant for us in our own age to recover it.

But we will come back to all this in due course.

*    *    *

Two things about the Gospel of John should be borne in mind, even if they seem to be somewhat in tension.

*First, the Gospel of John clearly has a historical basis.* This is — or should be — an unremarkable assertion, assuming, as internal evidence suggests, that the core of the Gospel is based on an eyewitness's "memoirs." There is little reason to doubt that events, characters, geography of the region previous to 70 AD (as confirmed by archaeology), sayings of Jesus, and other details are based on fact. We have indications from the first three centuries that some Christian writers even preferred the chronology of John to that of the other Gospels.

Regarding the astounding works of Jesus recounted in John, and no matter how embroidered these may be, there are no historical grounds to question whether or not Jesus was a worker of wonders. John's miracle accounts (referred to as "signs" — *semeia* — , and seven in number), at their most basic, remind us just how stunning Jesus' deeds must have been.

But, if John is *based* on history, we nevertheless must recognize, if we are to understand the import of the work, that John is not merely a recorder of history. He is doing something more than that.

So, *second, we can reasonably say that the Gospel is a mytho-poeic work.* By that I mean, not that John is a work of fiction, but that *interwoven* throughout the narrative are symbolic or iconic elements, as mentioned above. I use the word *interwoven* intentionally, because this is one of the terms used in the third century by Origen to explain how John's Gospel was made up of history, carefully devised literary language, and narrative elaboration; and this interweaving was done in order to bring into bold relief the spiritual import of the work. Although a twenty-first-century student of biblical literature cannot follow Origen in all his third-century methods of interpretation and their conclusions (which often stretch allegorical explanations of numerous passages to excess), still one can be amazed at the sophisticated insight into biblical composition that Origen (and others, both Jewish and Christian) possessed during these early ages.

Never is this more the case than in his bold explanation of what the Gospels, as sacred literature, were intended to accomplish for their readers. "Anyone who will read [the Gospels] with attention," writes Origen in one place, "... will observe that in those narratives which appear to be literally recorded, there are inserted and interwoven things which cannot be admitted historically, but which may be accepted in a spiritual signification."[3] In his *Commentary on John*, Origen straightforwardly says things that would be guaranteed to upset a modern-day biblical literalist, and yet his view reveals at least one stream of *ancient and classical* biblical interpretation:

> [The writers of the Gospels] made full use for their purpose of things done by Jesus in the exercise of his wonderful and extraordinary power; they use in the same way his sayings, and in some places they tack on to their writing, with language apparently implying things of sense, things made manifest to them in a purely intellectual way. I do not condemn them if they even some-

3. Origen, *De Principiis*, Bk. IV, Ch. 1, 16 (cf. *Ante-Nicene Fathers*, Vol. 4 [Peabody, MA: Hendrickson Publishers, 1999], p. 365). For an engrossing discussion of Origen's and other early Fathers' exegeses of the Gospels (unfortunately long out of print), one could not do better than search out and confer: Robert M. Grant, *The Earliest Lives of Jesus* (New York: Harper and Brothers Publishers, 1961).

times dealt freely with things which to the eye of history happened differently, and changed them so as to serve the mystical aims they had in view. . . . They proposed to speak the truth where it was possible both materially and spiritually, and where this was not possible it was their intention to prefer the spiritual to the material. The spiritual truth was often preserved, as one might say, in the material falsehood.[4]

We must be quick to make clear that Origen, and the other early Fathers holding this same view, were not saying that the Evangelists were making up things, but that they were consciously using what we today might call *poetic license*. They were framing the narrative in such a way that its significance would make an impact on the reader. Another analogy for this, as I have implied already, can be found in Eastern Christian iconography. Those familiar with this ancient form of art know that its depictions of persons and events are not meant to be simple renderings taken from history, much less "photographic" or realistic. They are stylized in such a way that an icon's inner meaning alters and shines through the scene or personage depicted. Icons are as much richly symbolic as historically

4. Origen, *Commentary on the Gospel of John*, Bk. X, Ch. 4 (cf. *Ante-Nicene Fathers*, Vol. 9 [Peabody, MA: Hendrickson Publishers, 1999], p. 383).

inspired — and in that sense they are somewhat like our written Gospels.

For Origen, reading John "with attention" means that we should read it with open minds to its deeper meaning. Otherwise, much of John will remain obscure, and we will miss a great deal of what this work is meant to communicate to us. In other words, *literalism* — just as surely as excessive allegorizing — can prove to be a hindrance to understanding what a Gospel conveys. John is not concerned about writing a biography or even something like a hagiography; he is concerned about presenting the spiritual truth of Christ's coming. This means that the author, in the words of Origen, preferred "the spiritual to the material." Or, to put it another way, the Gospel of John was always, right from the very beginning, intended to be first and foremost *a work of spiritual awakening*, not a simple rendition of facts.

To press on, John is most evidently "mythopoeic" in the following two complementing ways.

First, the Gospel takes as its mythical framework and occasional foil the first three chapters of Genesis. The themes of cosmic creation (Genesis 1), the creation of man and woman and their placement in the garden (Genesis 2), and the "fall" (Genesis 3) are all "interwoven" into this Gospel, right from the identical openings of Genesis and John

("In the beginning"), to the image of man and woman and two angels in a garden near the Gospel's conclusion. John undoubtedly intended to mirror (and reverse) the narratives in Genesis 1–3, all the while reinterpreting the language of Genesis in the light of Jesus.

Second, John will create a unique mythopoeic portrait of Jesus. To give an example of this, and as noted above already, Jesus performed many "signs" throughout his ministry, many of them not recorded in the Gospel (as John acknowledges: 20:30-31); but John tells of seven important signs that stand out as especially indicative of Jesus' identity. These are: the transformation of water into wine at the wedding feast at Cana (2:1-11), the curing of a Gentile nobleman's son (4:46-54), the curing of a paralytic (5:1-18), the feeding of the multitude (6:6-13), Jesus walking on the water (6:16-21), the curing of the man born blind (9:1-7), and the raising of Lazarus from the dead (11:1-45). There are other instances of this sort of creative reshaping of Jesus' ministry by John, but this sevenfold "book of signs" (as some scholars have called chapters 2–11) indicates that the Gospel has been carefully structured.

These two forms of mythopoeicism are at work in John, and they are there to bring the reader to a personal revelation of who Christ is — "that believing you may have life in his name" (20:31).

⋆ ⋆ ⋆

In the pages that follow I will take a handful of John's most significant words — "woman," "hour," and "garden" in particular, but others besides that have bearing on these three — and explore their implications. This book is both a literary analysis and a spiritual reflection. For a Gospel that opens with the line "In the beginning was the Word," these things — literary analysis and spiritual reflection — can certainly be said to hold together. It is my hope that in teasing out at least some of the "code" that is threaded throughout John's work, we will discover anew old aspects of who we are in union with God in Christ.

# TWO

# EXCURSUS: THE "VIRGIN MOTHER" IN CHRISTIAN TYPOLOGY

The Madonna with Joseph and Five Angels (c. 1505)

IT IS WITH the image of "the Woman" in John, both as archetype (16:21) and as reflected in three types in the text (the Mother of Christ, the woman of Samaria, and Mary Magdalene), that this book is most centrally concerned. The case I will make is that "the Woman" is an icon of the gathered community (and the individual local communities) of disciples. That is to say, it represents the church as an organism living in union with God through Christ, and that the church — viewed collectively — is the "bride" of the "Bridegroom" (John 3:29) and the "mother" of the baptized (cf. 2 John 1, 13). That is a lot to take in at the outset, admittedly, but it will be the object of the remainder of this book to explore the claim at length.

In this chapter, though, I wish to look at the image of "the Woman" as it was given definitive iconic shape in the person of Mary, the virgin mother of Christ. We will fail to understand the role she has played historically within the tradition, iconography, devotion, and liturgies of the church, East and West, if we fail to make the connection between her image and the biblical typology of the church as "Woman." It is the latter that created "Mariology," and not the historical mother of Jesus apart from that matrix of early Christian symbolism.

When the ancient church "saw" the Virgin Mother of Christ, depicted in art or celebrated in the prayers, what was it that she saw? To answer the question directly, she saw *herself* in the image of Mary.

The foundations for this had been laid in the Scriptures, first in the Old Testament prophets, in which the people of Judah and Israel and "mother" Jerusalem were described as the espoused bride of God, often with her children in tow. (See, for example, such texts as Isaiah 54:1-17; Jeremiah 2:2; the parable of Ezekiel 16; and Hosea 2:1-23.) The Song of Songs was included in the canon by the rabbis precisely because this collection of erotic poems was read "spiritually," as being a book celebrating the love between God and his people. This theme of a "virgin" who is espoused to God and is the "mother" of his "children" is picked up by the New Testament writers and applied to the church — which (as we shall see) was understood to be the continuation of "the people of God." Paul, for example, wrote to the church in Corinth that he had betrothed them "as a chaste virgin to Christ" (2 Cor. 11:2), and he described the "Jerusalem above" (a spiritualized vision of the Old Testament prophets' "mother Jerusalem") as "the mother of us all" (Gal. 4:26). So it was that the early church already held a tradition-informed understanding of her ideal identity as that of "Virgin Mother." She was a "virgin" espoused to Christ; she was a "mother" in bringing many children spiritually to birth. This is why the Epistle to the Ephesians, when referring to

Christian marriage, sees in it much more than a simple nuptial contract between a man and a woman. It becomes the "icon" of Christ's union with his church, indeed a revelation of a "profound" eschatological "mystery": "'For this reason a man shall leave his father and mother and be joined to his wife, and the two shall become one flesh.' This mystery is a profound one, and I am saying that it refers to Christ and the church . . ." (Eph. 5:31-32; cf. Gen. 2:24).

One image in the New Testament that could only be opaque to us, unless understood in light of the above, is that of the "woman clothed with the sun" in Revelation 12. Early Christians did not draw too sharp a distinction between the Old Testament church and the New Testament church. For them, the "church" had its origin in the very beginning, with the first pair in Eden. It was reconstituted, after failure upon failure, with the calling of Abraham (Genesis 12) — a point made, for instance, by Paul in such texts as Galatians 3:6-9. Indeed, so much is it the case that the Christian "church" is a continuation of the Old Covenant "church," that Paul does not hesitate to warn Gentile believers in Christ not to "boast" when comparing themselves with Jewish believers. Using the metaphor that there is a single "olive tree" into which they have been "grafted" through baptism, he tells them: "remember it is not you who support the root, but the root that supports you" (Rom. 11:18).

From the perspective of the New Testament, then, a sharp disjuncture between the Old Testament community and the community of Christ is not entirely clear or obvious. A new dispensation had been revealed with the coming of Christ, the doors had been opened to receive the Gentiles among the people of God (as the Old Testament prophets had predicted), but none of these things were essentially a repudiation of "the church" which had existed from the beginning. So, whereas Paul had used the analogy of an olive tree, the book of Revelation describes the vision of "a woman clothed with the sun" who is "with child" and "cried out in pangs of birth" (Gen. 3:17 and John 16:21!). Her child is Christ, who is to rule all nations and who is "caught up to God and to his throne" (a veiled reference, it seems, to his resurrection and ascension). In the vision, the woman flees into the wilderness to escape the dragon (who is identified as Satan, the "ancient serpent" of Eden; 12:9). Lastly, the seer tells his readers, "[T]he dragon was angry with the woman, and went off to make war on the rest of her offspring, on those who keep the command-ments of God and bear testimony to Jesus" (Rev. 12:1-2, 5-6, 9, 13, 17). Here, in the striking symbol of a heavenly and preexistent "woman," we have both the "mother" of Christ and the "mother" of other offspring — those who are, in fact, Jesus' disciples. In the mind of the writer of the book of Revelation, no clear distinction exists between the heavenly Israel/Jerusalem as "mother" of Jesus and the church as the "mother" of Jesus' disciples. There is only one "mother" and one archetypal "woman." Because of this long-ingrained idea, Augustine (354-430) could write, in a passage about the virgin mother Mary: "[T]he Church is the mother of Christ."[1]

That the Christian community had been, from its inception, traditionally symbolized as a virgin bride and mother, and continued to be through the millennia, is everywhere evident in the tradition. To cite one of the earliest of the writings of the "Apostolic Fathers" as an example (so called because these writings represent the second generation of the earliest Christians, some of them even included in early biblical canons in the various churches), *The Shepherd of Hermas*, written in Rome in the second century, depicts the church as an ancient lady who grows ever younger throughout a series of visions. One cannot truly appreciate patristic and medieval devotion to the Blessed Virgin Mary without understanding that she — the Virgin and Mother who gave birth to the historical "body of Christ" — was viewed early on as the preeminent icon of

1. Augustine, *Sermo Denis* 25, 8, quoted in Luigi Gambero, *Mary and the Fathers of the Church: The Blessed Virgin in Patristic Thought* (San Francisco: Ignatius Press, 1999), p. 223.

the church. Again, in the words of Augustine, "Indeed, the Church also is both virgin and mother, mother because of her womb of charity, virgin because of the integrity of her faith and piety."[2]

The texts are well beyond counting in patristic and medieval sources that liken the church to Mary. Hugo Rahner, in his classic, readable little study of patristic thought regarding Mary as icon of the church, could simply write: "This is the fundamental doctrine, that Mary is a type or symbol of the Church, and therefore everything that we find in the Gospel about Mary can be understood in a proper biblical sense of the mystery of the Church."[3] Henri de Lubac could write much the same thing: "Everywhere the Church finds in [Mary] her type and model, her point of origin and perfection: 'The form of our Mother the Church is according to the form of his Mother.' Our Lady speaks and acts in the name of the Church at every moment of her existence . . . because she already carries the Church within her, so to speak, and contains her, in her wholeness, in her own

---

2. Augustine, *Sermo Denis* 192, 2, quoted in Gambero, *Mary and the Fathers of the Church*, p. 223.

3. Hugo Rahner, S.J., *Our Lady and the Church*, trans. Sebastian Bullough, O.P. (Chicago: H. Regnery, 1965; reprint: Bethesda, MD: Zaccheus Press, 2004), p. 13. Unless otherwise noted, the patristic and medieval quotations in this chapter can be found in this slim and helpful volume.

person."[4] De Lubac is merely echoing the view of numerous Fathers that Mary, as Mother of Christ, is also the Mother of Christ's body, the church. She is thus the preeminent image of the church (the *qahal*, the *ekklesia*, the assembly of God's elect) that began with the "yes" of Abraham (Genesis 12), the church that experienced her betrothal at the foot of Mount Sinai, and had (as Origen put it in his *Commentary on the Song of Songs*) the Old Testament prophets, culminating with John the Baptist, as "friends of the Bridegroom," who had prepared her for her marriage to the Incarnate Word. "The wife of Christ" ("the wife of the Lamb" — Rev. 21:9), wherever such a notion is present in ancient Christian literature and imagery, both orthodox and heterodox, is therefore never to be taken literally; from the outset the idea is iconographic in nature only, a metaphor, a spiritual depiction of the loving relationship between Christ and his gathered community.

Mary was also at times, though much less often, associated with the Old Testament personification of Wisdom. It is the "wise" person, after all, who *receives* the implantation of God's Word, and every Christian is called to be a wise disciple (and thus a true "child" of the virgin mother church). One can see why Origen would mention her in relation to

4. Henri de Lubac, *The Splendor of the Church*, trans. Michael Mason (San Francisco: Ignatius Press, 1986), p. 320.

taking in the "wisdom" contained in the Gospel of John: "No one can apprehend the meaning of it except he have lain on Jesus' breast and received from Jesus Mary to be his mother also."[5]

The word "wisdom" is feminine in gender in Hebrew, Greek, and Latin, and so is the word "soul," and Mary is aptly an image of the "wise soul," the wise disciple who gives birth to Christ within her. In this way she not only represents the community of faith, but also the faithful member of that community. The twelfth-century Cistercian Father Isaac of Stella, picking up this slim patristic thread, could thus write: "Whatever is said of God's eternal wisdom itself, can be applied in a wide sense to the Church, in a narrower sense to Mary, and in a particular way to every faithful soul."[6] Likewise, another Cistercian of the twelfth and thirteenth centuries, Adam of Perseigne, wrote:

"Who shall find a valiant woman? Far from the uttermost coasts is the price of her" (Prov. 31:10). . . . [S]urely we can understand that the valiant woman is the wisdom of God, either Mary, the mother of Wisdom itself [because she is the mother of Christ, the eternal Word], or the Church,

---

5. Origen, *Commentary on the Gospel of John*, Bk. 1, Ch. 6 (cf. *Ante-Nicene Fathers*, Vol. 9 [Peabody, MA: Hendrickson Publishers, 1999], p. 300).

6. Isaac of Stella, *Sermo* 51, on the Assumption.

mother of the wise, or, certainly, the soul as the seat of
wisdom. God's wisdom is called a woman because of the
fruitfulness of all good things that flow from her. For it is
she who announces: "I am the mother of fair love, and of
fear, and of knowledge, and of holy hope." (Sirach 24:24)[7]

Mary's wisdom was, of course, plainly visible in the biblical account. She had "kept all these things and pondered
them in her heart . . . his mother kept all these things in
her heart" (Luke 2:19, 51). She was, then, an icon of holy
wisdom, pondering the mysteries of revelation. It was
never lost on the mind of the church, visible in art and devotion throughout the Christian centuries, that Mary had
conceived Jesus within her through her willing reception
of the Word of God at the Annunciation. "Mary kept the
words of Christ in her heart," wrote Origen, "kept them as
a treasure, knowing that the time would come, when all that
was hidden within her would be unveiled."[8] In a lesser way,
as many of the Fathers — prominent among them Gregory Nazianzen and Gregory of Nyssa — asserted, Christ is
conceived in our souls and so is born within us. Ambrose
of Milan could say, for instance: "When the soul then be-

7. Adam of Perseigne, "Sermon 5, On the Assumption," trans. Philip
O'Mara, *Cistercian Studies Quarterly* 33, no. 2 (1998): 152.
8. Origen, *Homily on Luke*, 20.

gins to turn to Christ, she is addressed as 'Mary,' that is, she receives the name of the woman who bore Christ in her womb: for she has become a soul who in a spiritual sense gives birth to Christ."[9] In the words of Augustine: "When you look with wonder on what happened to Mary, you must imitate her in the depths of your own souls. Whoever believes with all his heart and is 'justified by faith' (Rom. 5:1), he has conceived Christ in the womb; and whenever 'with the mouth confession is made unto salvation' (Rom. 10:10), that man has given birth to Christ."[10]

★      ★      ★

There is much more that could be written about this rich subject, and the sources for discussion are plenteous; but I have only ventured on this excursus here, so early in this book, to make a simple point. That point is this: the image of "the Woman," as we will find it embedded in the Johannine writings, had its origins in the Hebrew canon that preceded the Christian revelation, and it has continued in the tradition of the church to this day. When we see, for instance, an icon of the Theotokos in the churches of the East or hear someone saying the "Hail Mary" before a

9. Ambrose of Milan, *De Virginitate* 4, 20.
10. Augustine, *Sermo* 191, 4.

statue of the Blessed Virgin in the West, we see the continuation of that ancient tradition. It has often been literalized, concretized, and rendered opaque as simply a devotion to a person, and that has tended to reduce the power of the icon as icon, and mute its inherent meaning for us. And, as we shall see, too, Mary is not the only image of "the Woman" in John's Gospel (or elsewhere in early Christian literature). But, having said all that, it is striking that this icon is still with us, though sometimes unrecognized, and often mistaken as something "extra-biblical" instead of — as it is — profoundly biblical.

Lastly, with that contemporary interest in the pestering question of whether or not Jesus was married before us, we can give an answer to it here and now. Yes, he was and is "married." His "wife" is the community of the faithful, and the church has always known the identity of Jesus' "wife," even if many (both outside and within her) have forgotten it.

There is no reason to doubt that Jesus, literally and historically, was never married. Celibacy had been the lot of such Old Testament prophets as Elijah, Elisha, Jeremiah, and Daniel. It was practiced among the Essenes in Jesus' day; and, in the New Testament, we find that John the Baptist, Paul, Barnabas, James the brother of the Lord, and others were not married. Jesus was aflame with prophetic zeal, and that often meant that the one so aflame with the urgency of a divinely ordained mission was a celibate man. One need not even presuppose (as certainly this author does) the divinity of Christ to presuppose his celibate status. But it has also always been presupposed by the church that he is a "married man" — married, that is, spiritually and fully to his people.

# THREE

# "THE WOMAN" AND THE WOMEN ADDRESSED AS "WOMAN" IN JOHN

*Christ Taking Leave of His Mother* (c. 1509-1511)

I F THERE IS a "key" biblical text to this short volume, it is the enigmatic saying of Jesus to his disciples in John 16:21. It is spoken within the context of the portion of the Gospel known as the "Farewell Discourse," which stretches through the course of three entire chapters (14, 15, and 16), culminating with the lengthy prayer of Jesus that comprises chapter 17. In context, the saying is meant to be a word of comfort. Jesus informs the disciples that, although he will be taken from them through his death on the cross and they will experience sorrow for a short while, they will know lasting joy through his resurrection.

The saying in 16:21 may serve a simple purpose, but its phraseology is anything but simple. In fact, it contains a number of features that are allusive and, frankly, "mystical" in tone. It is a bit like an onion, one might say; it will prove to be the sort of text that one can continue to peel down layer by layer. That is a feature I must return to in due course, but here I give my own literal rendering of the text from the Greek. I have put a few words in bold type — first, because they are faithful to the Greek wording (in a way that many translations, unfortunately, are not); and, second, because a literal rendering is so important to the deeper meaning that any other rendering than the literal does a disservice to the text. Here is the verse:

When **the woman** [note the definite article here] is in travail she has sorrow, because **her hour** has come; but when she is delivered of the child, she no longer remembers the anguish, for joy that a **man** [*anthropos*] is born into the world.

At this point I will ask only that you keep in mind that the verse refers to "*the* Woman," and not to *a* woman — the definite article is not irrelevant, as some translations imply by dropping it; also that the verse makes reference to "*her* hour"; and, lastly, that the child "born into the world" (itself a significant phrase in John) is called "a man" (*anthropos*), that is to say, a *human being* (not "a child" or "a baby").

Leaving open the question of the significance of 16:21 for the moment, which will be a central concern of this book, we find that in John's Gospel Jesus deliberately addresses three different women in four distinct passages as "Woman." One might see nothing particularly unusual in two of these instances — at one time he addresses the Samaritan woman and at another he addresses Mary Magdalene. Neither woman can be said to hold a status deserving of special honorific language from him. The third person so addressed, however, is his own mother, whom he calls "Woman" twice — once in chapter 2 and again in chapter 19. If the first two instances seem unremarkable, the same cannot be said of the third. This address, as we shall see, has bothered and even scandalized pious readers for ages. Why would a son address his own mother simply as "Woman" — not the norm in any age, and certainly not one in Jesus' day? I believe we should see this enigmatic address as somehow related to the equally enigmatic text of 16:21, with its reference to "the Woman." (There is another instance of the use of the address "Woman" by Jesus for yet a fourth woman — the woman taken in adultery. However, the entire passage in which it appears, 7:53–8:11, is a later addition to the Gospel. So, although it is an interesting supplement, it falls outside our consideration here.)

I turn my attention, then, to those four instances of Jesus addressing the three women as "Woman," and — taking them somewhat out of order at the outset — I look first at John 19:25-28. I take it first because, along with 16:21, it has a special, vital, and mystical meaning within the Gospel. The passage, John 19:25-28, is the second time that Jesus addresses his mother with the term, the first time being at the wedding feast of Cana in chapter 2 (see below). The reader will note that I have again put two words in bold type. These words are "Woman" and "hour," both words having appeared already in 16:21.

19:25 . . . But standing by the cross of Jesus were his mother, and his mother's sister, Mary the wife of Clopas, and Mary

Magdalene. ²⁶When Jesus saw his mother, and the disciple whom he loved standing near, he said to his mother, "**Woman**, behold, your son!" ²⁷Then he said to the disciple, "Behold, your mother!" And from that **hour** the disciple took her to his own home. ²⁸After this Jesus, knowing that all was now finished, said (to fulfil the scripture), "I thirst."

The astute reader of John will already know that the word "hour" *(hora)* shows up at significant places in the Gospel, and sometimes in proximity to the word "Woman" *(gyne)*. Whenever there is reference in John to "the hour" which is "coming," or whenever Jesus refers to "my hour," the word takes on a weight of meaning. Numerous verses, besides those already mentioned (16:21 and 19:27), mention this "hour": 5:25-30; 7:30; 8:20; 12:23-28; 13:1; 16:32; and 17:1. Likewise, Jesus also uses the word "time" *(kairos)* in a way that seems synonymous with "hour" in 7:6-8. In John, "the hour" and "time" that is "coming" is specified as that of Jesus' "glorification." Paradoxically, his "glorification" corresponds to the time of his crucifixion, when his mission in the world is "accomplished" (19:30). The cross is his "glory" — itself a tremendous revelation of God's love (cf. 1 John 4:9-10). "The hour" includes in its embrace, as well, his departure from the world and the scattering of his disciples; but, more, it also embraces the resurrection. It is "the hour" of salvation, and as such it perdures as a present reality. The "hour" of the crucifixion-resurrection is the perpetual source and spring of new life for humankind. It is the hour of our resurrection spiritually (cf. 5:25-26), the font of our new birth (cf. 3:3-8). We can say suggestively at this early stage, in fact, that it is when a *new* "man is born into the world."

Looking, then, at those other three passages in which Jesus uses the address "Woman," we note that the word "hour" also appears in the first two cited below.

Jesus addresses his mother:

2:2Jesus also was invited to the marriage, with his disciples. 3When the wine failed, the mother of Jesus said to him, "They have no wine." 4And Jesus said to her, "O **woman**, what have you to do with me? My **hour** has not yet come."

Jesus addresses the Samaritan woman:

4:21Jesus said to her, "**Woman**, believe me, the **hour** is coming when neither on this mountain nor in Jerusalem will you worship the Father. 22You worship what you do not know; we worship what we know, for salvation is from the Jews. ²³But the **hour** is coming, and now is, when the true worshipers will worship the Father in spirit and truth, for such the Father seeks to worship him.

Lastly, two angels and Jesus address Mary Magdalene outside the garden tomb, after the resurrection of Jesus:

> ²⁰:¹¹But Mary stood weeping outside the tomb, and as she wept she stooped to look into the tomb; ¹²and she saw two angels in white, sitting where the body of Jesus had lain, one at the head and one at the feet. ¹³They said to her, **"Woman**, why are you weeping?" She said to them, "Because they have taken away my Lord, and I do not know where they have laid him." ¹⁴Saying this, she turned round and saw Jesus standing, but she did not know that it was Jesus. ¹⁵Jesus said to her, **"Woman**, why are you weeping? Whom do you seek?"

Undoubtedly the three women in the passages above are to be understood as unique, individual, and historical persons. John is not prone to flat allegorizing. He is a subtle and poetic writer. All three women are delicately and deftly delineated with psychological insight. But John, we may assume, has also intentionally put the word "Woman" on Jesus' lips in his version of events, apparently in order to signify a specific *something else* we are meant to catch, something else that shines through each of these distinct women like refracted light. So, what might the importance of "Woman" be as an address? It may well be that "the Woman" in 16:21 is an archetype, in relation to which these three specific women stand as types. It is "the Woman" — whoever she is — that we are meant to see shining in the "icons" of these three particular women.

It has troubled pious exegetes, as I mentioned above, that Jesus addresses his mother in John 2 in such a seemingly discourteous way. After all, this is his mother; and if we are Catholics, Orthodox, Anglicans, or Christians of any other tradition that extols Mary, we cannot easily picture Jesus speaking to the Blessed Virgin so disrespectfully.

But such considerations very likely miss John's real point. This Gospel, we must recall, never even divulges the name of Jesus' mother. In John's Gospel, she is never once referred to as "Mary." *Something else* is going on here, something "iconographic," although it clearly has an embryonic relationship to later piety surrounding Christ's mother.

Just to clarify the matter a bit more, there are only three possible ways to understand Jesus' designation of his mother as "Woman."

Either

(1) this is indeed a distancing or even rude address, or

(2) it is some sort of endearment or respectful term for her, or

(3) the term has a symbolic purpose.

We can dismiss the first two possibilities with little effort:

(1) First, although Jesus' words to his mother do distance him from her (literally, he says, "Woman, what is there between me and you?"), there is no justification for thinking the address is meant to be rude. That he addresses her again in exactly the same fashion, as we saw above, while he is on the cross, there seeing to her comfort and care after his departure (19:26), should make it sufficiently evident that his use of "Woman" for her in chapter 2 is not meant to be a belittlement of her either. If its use is not disrespectful in 19:26, then it is not disrespectful in 2:4.

(2) But, on the other hand, could Jesus in this context possibly mean the address as nearly the exact opposite of belittlement, as instead a sort of endearment? One frankly inane translation has even rendered it as "dear lady"; and

the Revised Standard Version, which I have reluctantly quoted verbatim above, renders it ever so politely as "O woman." But there is no "O" in the original Greek verse, nor "dear," nor even the word "lady" (which would, as in English, be a different word in Greek — a point we shall return to below); there is just the address "Woman." Quite simply, Jesus is not using the term as an endearment.

(3) So, we are left with only the third possible reason for using this odd address as being the most credible one: the Gospel means to suggest something figurative by it. And, if this is so for Jesus' mother, it is probable that the same is true for both the Samaritan woman and Mary Magdalene when Jesus addresses them in like fashion.

So, then, how might these three women, when addressed as "Woman," be related in John's thinking to "the Woman" of 16:21? And what is it that "the Woman" represents?

If we look at the immediate context of John 16:21, especially noting the verses that precede and follow it (vv. 20 and 22), we see that Jesus is speaking to *his disciples* about the "sorrow" that they will undergo at his departure, and of the later joy that they will feel when they see him again. The entire passage reads as follows:

> 16:20Truly, truly, I say to you, you will weep and lament, but the world will rejoice; you will be sorrowful, but your

sorrow will turn into joy. ²¹When the woman is in travail she has sorrow, because her hour has come; but when she is delivered of the child, she no longer remembers the anguish, for joy that a man is born into the world. ²²So you have sorrow now, but I will see you again and your hearts will rejoice, and no one will take your joy from you.

To speak to the feelings of *sorrow* that the disciples will feel at the time of Jesus' crucifixion, Jesus presents the image of "the Woman" in travail — "she has sorrow, because her hour has come." Two aspects of this passage and its context are deserving of our attention. The first thing to mark is that "the sorrow" and "joy" of "the Woman" are emblematic of the sorrow and joy of *the disciples.* That is to say, *those* whose approaching sorrow and joy are being addressed by Jesus' words are crucial for our understanding of the identity of "the Woman" in the verse. The second thing to note is that the woman's travail is that of *childbirth.* She is bringing a new life into "the world" *(kosmos).* It is the birth of "a man" *(anthropos).* To put it succinctly, the Woman's "hour" is the hour when she gives birth to a new man.

Given these clues, who then is "the Woman"? We should not miss the detail that the Woman (with her child) is directly identified with Christ's disciples — in other words, with "the church." Looking back to our brief discussion above of the development of Marian piety, with its roots in the Old Testament's bridal analogy for the gathered people of God (the "church"), and the continuation of that same analogy in the New Testament and the early Fathers, we can with no trouble recognize in John's analogy of "the Woman" and her child an exalted image of the "assembly" of disciples themselves. It is not too great a stretch to suggest that "the Woman" and her child comprise a single image of Jesus' (and John's) community or "church."

Is there any evidence in the writings of John to suggest that the whole community of Jesus' followers was ever conceived of as "feminine" and symbolized as a "Woman" with "children" (the "children" being individual baptized — that is, *reborn* — members)? This is a necessary question to pose, if we would advance the notion we have already put forward. Well, in point of fact, and as scant as it may be, *there is such evidence.* It stands out for us in the Second Letter of John. There we read the following:

> The elder to the **elect lady** and her **children**, whom I love in the truth, and not only I but also all who know the truth, because of the truth which abides in us and will be with us for ever: Grace, mercy, and peace will be with us, from God the Father and from Jesus Christ the Father's Son, in truth and love. I rejoiced greatly to find some of your **children**

following the truth, just as we have been commanded by the Father. And now I beg you, **lady**, not as though I were writing you a new commandment, but the one we have had from the beginning, that we love one another. (2 John 1–5)

And the same letter concludes with these words: "The **children** of your **elect sister** greet you" (2 John 13).

The word translated "Lady" in these verses is an honorific term, *kyria*. It is the feminine equivalent of "Lord" — *kyrios*. There seems little doubt that the "elect Lady" and her "children" represent the community to whom "the elder" is writing in 2 John, and "the children of your elect sister" is a reference to the individual members of the local community from which he writes. There are, in other words, two "Ladies" indicated — that is to say, two "congregations" or local churches — that are "sisters" with "children" they have borne. These two "Ladies" share a single archetype: an honored Woman who is surrounded by children to whom she has given birth (we have already seen something similar in our brief discussion of Revelation 12 in the last chapter).

An "icon" of the Christian (or, at least, Johannine) community, it appears, was precisely this image of an extended family. The Bridegroom and Lord would, in this analogy, be the Son (cf. John 3:29), and the seed-giving Father would, of course, be God (cf. 1 John 3:9-10). Each community would be a "sister" among "sisters," each with her own children gathered about her — a plurality of "Ladies," yet sharing one archetype; each dignified as a "Lady" and regarded as a "sister" of equal dignity with all the rest. The high title, kyria, would be indicative of the high spiritual nobility each community possessed through union with its Kyrios. The "children" of the "elect Lady" and her "elect sister," one can assume, were those who were baptized and reborn disciples.

If "the Woman" of John 16:21 is the archetypal image of the church, and if the address "Woman," used of three separate women in the Gospel, points to that archetype, it is just possible that "the elect Lady" and her "elect sister" in 2 John are the development of that same image. There is more than one woman addressed in the Gospel, yet all three represent "the Woman" (who is the church). There is more than one "Lady" mentioned in 2 John — a plurality of "sisters" — who are, nonetheless, local expressions of the one, united church.

But, with all that under our belts, there is more to this image of "the Woman" yet to explore, and this will take us deeper and further into John's mystical thought.

So far we have been skirting the edges of a garden. We will need to enter it, though, to make our way to "the tree in the midst of the garden."

# FOUR

# EXCURSUS: LIFE AND DEATH IN JOHN

*Christ on the Cross with the Virgin and St. John* (1510)

BEFORE RETURNING TO the theme of "the Woman" of 16:21, however, we will look at a topic that, although at first it may appear to be only tangentially related to the theme, lies actually at the heart of it. It is the subject of "eternal life," which in John is of paramount importance. If in the Synoptic Gospels Jesus proclaims "the kingdom of God," in John he proclaims himself as the way to sharing in the everlasting life of God. In all the writings of John, in fact, and in contrast to the many mentions of "eternal life," the phrase "the kingdom of God" appears only twice (John 3:3, 5), and Jesus refers to "my kingdom" once (John 18:36). When we compare the meager use of the phrase in John with the many times Jesus teaches at length about it in the other Gospels, we may wonder why there is such disparity.

In the Synoptic Gospels, the kingdom of God is the new order Jesus is bringing into being, one that will upset and invert the order of this world's "kingdoms." The Greek word translated as "kingdom" is *basileia*, and it could be translated "empire." The same Greek word was in fact used for the "kingdom" — or "empire" — of Rome, and Jesus is boldly contrasting God's empire with those of men. The kingdom of God, as Jesus teaches, is inaugurated by him personally and is made present here and now in seed form, and in the age to come it will be fully realized. On the practical level, "the kingdom of God" is intended to be an order of behavior and belief; it is the *way of life* Jesus expects his disciples to adopt if they want to follow him. So it is that he gives many practical teachings on how to live accordingly here and now.

But John, for his part, departs from this terminology and rarely mentions "the kingdom of God." As most scholars point out, the concept that replaces it in his Gospel and Epistles is that of "eternal life" *(zoen aionion)*. Casual readers may assume that "eternal life" means simply "immortality" and is to be equated with "heaven." Similarly, many — if not most — readers may read the familiar words of John 3:16 (that those who believe in the Son "should not perish but have eternal life") and jump to the conclusion that to "perish" means to be condemned to "hell." In a book I wrote a few years ago on the Sermon on the Mount, I had some short paragraphs on the subject of "hell," explaining that the various poetic images used by Jesus in the Synoptic Gospels referred mostly to one's own tragic self-wasting, self-loss, or self-exclusion. I will not repeat those observations here; but I will note that "hell" — literally "Gehenna" — is never brought up in John's writings at all. That is not an insignificant point. If a topic is never mentioned in a work written by a particular writer, it is reasonable to assume that it was not a topic uppermost in his mind. So, we are left with the following inferences regarding John's overall understanding of salvation: instead of the kingdom of God being the central message of Jesus in John, we find the promise of "eternal life" occupying that place; and, instead of a concept of "Gehenna" or "hell," we have the threat of "perishing," which is to say, the threat of ceasing to live.

Perhaps it is a long shot to say that John might be "de-mythologizing" the parallel concepts in the Synoptic Gospels. Even so, if we take "the kingdom of God" (in Matthew, Mark, and Luke) to be the parallel theme to "eternal life" (in John), and if in place of "Gehenna" John speaks of "perishing," then we can at least plausibly suggest that John is taking these ideas to a different and (I think) deeper level. He has stripped down the poetic imagery about damnation, as it appears in the Synoptics (fire, worms, outer darkness, etc.), and in its place he refers starkly to death and nonexistence. Whereas the Synoptics make use of the imagery of such texts as Isaiah 66:24 for ultimate self-loss, John uses the simpler language of such texts as Psalm 146:4: "When [man's] breath departs he returns to the earth; on that very day his plans [or "thoughts"] perish." We could say that the more profound level we find in John is more frankly ontological or existential, unvarnished and unpoeticized, bringing us directly to one of the most basic antinomies we face: *life* and *death*.

We find three Greek words meaning "life" used in the

writings of John, and each is used in a specific sense. Noting those distinctions is crucial when we seek a better understanding of what John means in those passages where our English translators had no option but to resort to using the one word "life."

First, there is the Greek word *bios*. John uses *bios* just once in the writings we have. *Bios* means "life" as it relates to what sustains it tangibly — the physical resources, wealth, provisions, etcetera, upon which we depend to maintain ourselves. In the single verse where it appears, it is used in a negative context. In 1 John 2:16, grouped along with "lust of the flesh" and "lust of the eyes," we have "the pride of *life*." This is a phrase referring to arrogance arising from power, prestige, property, or possessions. The word *bios* here means the "life" we make for ourselves or which causes us to have worldly success. It is material and physical, and tends towards luxury or status. The "self-made man," the person with a "lifestyle" to maintain, or an inheritance or a title, a person who has "come into his living" (to wax Dickensian for a moment) — this is the aspect of life that John's use of *bios* implies.

The second word for "life" used by John is *psyche*. It is sometimes translated "soul," and thus has acquired a meaning that is less "material" and more "spiritual" than the word itself actually means. *Psyche* can refer to animal or vegetal life — cabbages have "souls" as do kings. Bodily life is included in "the life of the soul," and *psyche* has everything to do with blood and flesh and sap and sinew. It is the *natural life*, drawn from the earth and one with the seasons and the soil. It is organic and spiritual, and can include both the material and the immaterial "orders" of being. When "the elder" writes to "the beloved Gaius" in 3 John 2, he prays for the latter's bodily health, adding, "I know that it is well with your soul [*psyche*]." It is the human *psychic* life that dies just like the rest of physical living things. Whenever there is mention of "laying down" one's "life" (e.g., John 10:11-18; 13:37-38; 15:13; 1 John 3:16), the word for the latter is invariably *psyche*. Earthly "psychic" life is mortal life. Its nature is to live its appointed course and finally die, making way for renewal and new lives, as part of the cycle of the created order. It is inevitable that it eventually must be "laid down." Only in Jesus' case, John informs us, can it be "taken again" and restored by the power of the one who lays it down (John 10:18).

With that in mind, then, consider John 12:25, where we find our second word for "life" conjoined to the third Greek word translated as "life": "He who loves his life [*psyche*] loses it, and he who hates his life [*psyche*] in this world will keep it for eternal life [*zoe*]." This verse is connecting how we live in this world with *a new and different kind of life* (zoe) that is bestowed upon us by God. And this brings us to the heart of what John means in his usage of the different words for "life."

Looking at this third (and crucial) word, zoe, we have a term that can refer to animal life (think of "zoology," for example, or to the four "living creatures" — or "animals" = zoa — in Rev. 4:6), and so it is not all that different in its literal meaning from psyche or even bios. But John (consistent with other New Testament writers) uses these three words differently, and does so consistently throughout his writings. So it is that he uses the word zoe only in reference to the uncreated, immortal life of God — or "eternal life." When we read John, we should be aware that every time zoe appears in the Greek text, it means divine or eternal life, and never mortal life.

This is the case even in John 1:4 — "In him was life [zoe], and the life [zoe] was the light of men [anthropon]" (and we should take note of the past tense in this verse). John 1:4 is not referring to our present, natural psychic lives but to an "eternal life" which we originally possessed in the beginning — but lost. John is picking up on the vocabulary of the Greek version of the book of Genesis in order to make an important point about Christ's purpose in taking flesh and coming into the world. John is intentionally taking his readers back to the first three chapters of Genesis, echoing the language of the Septuagint (Greek) version. With 1:4 he is indicating the creation of man (*anthropos*) as found in Genesis 2, where we find these vitally important words: "God formed man [*anthropos*] from the earth and breathed into his face the breath of life [*zoes*] and man [*anthropos*] became a living soul [*psychen zosan*]" (Gen. 2:7).

Three words, as the bracketed words above indicate, should spring out at us immediately, if we have been following our word studies thus far. First, there is *anthropos*, a word we should recall from our discussion of 16:21 in the previous chapter. The word means "human being." In John, we find that *anthropoi* are those who have sinned with "the world." In one place we read that Jesus does not put his "trust" in "men" because he knows their nature too well (2:24-25); and yet he has come to rescue "man" and "not to condemn the world." It is to an *anthropos* (the term is used, quite intentionally, of Nicodemus in 3:1) that Jesus proclaims the good news of "new birth" or "birth from above" to "everlasting life [*zoe*]" (3:3-21). Second, the word *psyche* — the life we share with all created nature, the life that comes naturally from "the earth" from which we were formed — is important to note, specifically because it denotes a life that is not eternal in scope. Third, *zoe* is crucial for its significance as indicating the *divine* element that was added to man's *psyche* when God first "breathed into" man's "face the breath of (divine) life." "Man" at that point became what the Greek version of Genesis calls a *psyche zosan* — a *zoe-psyche*, if you will. In other words, man — unlike all the other *psyche*-creatures — is that unique earthly being endowed with *divine* life at the beginning. And so John, picking up the language of Genesis, can tell us: "In (the Word) was *zoe-life*, and the *zoe-life* **was** the light of men [*anthropon*]."

We should pause for the moment and reflect on this, because it is one of the vital keys to understanding John. Why did the light of Christ need to come and appear in the darkness of this world, to use John's own words in the very first chapter of his Gospel? The answer — or part of the answer — is so that we might have restored to us the lost *zoe-life* that God intended that we *anthropoi* share with him in the beginning. As we have said, *zoe-life* is God's own life, an utterly *different kind* of "life" than the mortal one (*psyche*), which we have received from our natural birth. It is the uncreated, divine life that he "breathed" into the face of man, and which untrustworthy man forfeited. This is, then, the symbolic meaning of why Jesus likewise "breathed" his "Spirit" ("Breath") upon his followers in 20:22, after his resurrection. John, it should be evident, wishes his readers to pick up on the figurative connection with Genesis 2:7, and see in this action of the risen Christ a new beginning — a second genesis and rebirth — for *anthropoi.*

"The sin of the world" (John 1:29) is the term John uses for man's "going off course" (the actual meaning of the word "sin") to choose a lesser sort of life than a share in God's. As a result, to use the mythic language of Genesis, "the way to the Tree of Life [zoes]" was cut off (Gen. 3:24) and, with it, so was the way to zoe-life. *Anthropos* was now off-course, outside "the garden," surviving in a wilderness physically and mentally, an alien in his own earthly home, fearful of his fellow creatures, searching for what was lost in the dark, sometimes seeing it afar, sometimes even reaching a measure of true illumination through various byways, perplexed, directionless, mortal, and forced, Cain-like, to fashion a "world" according to his own dimmed lights. He was a *psyche* only now, like the rest of material creation; his destiny now was to perish like the rest of material creation. This is the picture of *anthropos* in "this world," a creature bedeviled and unsatisfied, a mortal with lingering intimations of immortality. One can see why John saw the opposite course to "eternal life" as, simply and starkly, "perishing" — that is to say, ceasing to exist.

This imagery from Genesis is therefore the backdrop for John's mythopoeic retelling of the story of Jesus. John depicts the human situation as an unsettled place between the world and God, between mendacity and truth, between life and death, and between desire and fulfillment.

⋆　　⋆　　⋆

When the Gospel of John refers to *zoe* as that which Christ has come to give "abundantly" (10:10), he means more than something to be believed, more than a "saving" doctrine or body of knowledge, more even than the fruit of a sacramental act. One can say that he "believes" (in the sense of "accepts") the content of a doctrinal claim. Further, one might have faith that one has received the grace of "eternal life" through baptism or the Eucharist. But if "eternal life" remains at the level of a "concept" or an idea, one has not yet fully grasped John's intent. In many churches we hear of being "born again" or "born anew" — language taken directly from John's Gospel (3:3-8; see 16:21) — and what this is taken to mean is some sort of public "acceptance" of Jesus as "personal Lord and Savior." But believing that a *formula* is expressive of truth (whether it is that of the historic creeds or the Sinner's Prayer) is not to be taken as the *substance* of that truth. The meaning of the phrase "born again" for John has to do with the *reality* of ongoing communal experience and individual discipleship. There can be no doubt that what John means by "born again" begins with the external act of baptism (3:5, 22; 4:1-2), and it has everything to do with "belief" or "faith" — in the sense of one's personal investment of loyal "trust." But John means, above all, the awakening to an awareness of, and a continual growth in, the dynamic and everlasting gift of *zoe*. To be "born anew" is to enter into *zoe*, the life of the Spirit or "Breath" of God, and thus begin a deepening experience and an altered perception of every-thing. It is intended to be an expansion and transcending of the life of *psyche*, and with it there also comes the realization that the world is "passing away" (1 John 2:15-17).

We should assume that John's church was, in fact, a community of mystical participation, not merely a "church" as we usually think of it today — no pews, vestments, ad-ministrative headquarters, and so on. A community of dis-ciples, united under the spiritual oversight of wise elders (think rabbis, or even "gurus"), with a liturgy rich in mysti-cal symbolism, would not have been unusual for a religious association in that age. Mystical practices were likely part of his church's life. (Both contemporary Jewish and Greek mysticism influenced early Christianity.) The language of "rebirth" and "eternal life" would have meant more than simple doctrinal assent. It was something that the commu-nity experienced in their shared life, and that life would have been rigorous in its moral guidelines, commitment, and forms of worship. A "loose" community in matters of faith and practice could not have endured for long.

As we have already had occasion to remark, a common term for members of John's community was "children" —

indicating those who are born into a defined "family" and are learning and growing together. Let us look (again) at those verses in the Gospel that refer to this "rebirth" of the "children of God":

> Jesus answered [Nicodemus], "Truly, truly, I say to you, unless one is **born anew**, he cannot see the kingdom of God." Nicodemus said to him, "How can a man be born when he is old? Can he enter a second time into his mother's womb and be born?" Jesus answered, "Truly, truly, I say to you, unless one is **born of water and the Spirit**, he cannot enter the kingdom of God. **That which is born of the flesh is flesh, and that which is born of the Spirit is spirit.** Do not marvel that I said to you, 'You must be **born anew**.' The wind [or "Spirit" or "Breath"] blows where it wills, and you hear the sound of it, but you do not know whence it comes or whither it goes; so it is with every one who is **born of the Spirit**." (3:3-8)

And, once again:

> When the woman is in travail she has sorrow, because her hour has come; but when she is delivered of the child, she no longer remembers the anguish, for joy that a man is **born into the world.** (16:21)

And to these two passages, let me add this, for reasons that will immediately be made clear below:

He said to [the Pharisees], "You are from below, I am **from above**; you are of this world, I am not of this world. I told you that you would die in your sins, for you will die in your sins unless you believe that I am he." (8:23-24)

The Greek word for "anew" or "again" in the passage from John 3 is *ano*. Not only does the word mean "again," but it also means "above." So, when Jesus later says to the Pharisees that he is "from above," the word used is also *ano* (8:23-24). In that same passage in chapter 8 we have a strong assertion of Jesus' divinity, which will reach its climactic moment in verse 58: "Before Abraham was, I am." If we render 8:24 literally, it in fact reads: "You will die in your sins unless you trust that *I am*." We should read this latter verse as a plea to trust in the "grace and truth" that Jesus makes available (1:17). The bleak alternative is "dying in their sins," having missed the eternal life Christ offers. For, although God ("I am") cannot be seen in his invisible divine nature, he can be "known" through his Word made visible flesh (1:18). In other words, the one *"from above"* is offering his hearers *zoe-life* in place of *"dying in their sins"* — he is offering them, as he offers Nicode-

68

mus in a far less heated exchange, the possibility of being "born *from above.*"

Looking back at the dialogue between Jesus and Nicodemus in John 3, then, we should take note of the ambiguity in the term "born anew" or "born from above," an ambiguity John utilizes to his advantage. Nicodemus certainly takes it as meaning being born "a second time," and asks, perhaps a bit facetiously, "How can a man be born when he is old? Can he enter a second time into his mother's womb and be born?" But Jesus — or, rather, John, who renders it in Greek — means both "anew" and "from above." The beauty of poetic language is that a double meaning is always welcome. John doesn't want us to choose between the two possible meanings of *ano,* but to take them both together.

"Anew" suggests, as Jesus says explicitly, that there are two kinds of "birth" that one must have: "That which is born of the flesh is flesh, and that which is born of the Spirit is spirit." The first sort of birth is that which begins in the flesh through physical union and brings about the natural and mortal *psyche-life.* Jesus means that that which is born of the flesh is "flesh *only*" — in other words, it will live out its natural existence and then it will die. It is *essentially* perishable. *Psyche-life* is not inherently immortal; but *zoe-life* is. And, for one to have the latter, one must receive, as did the first man, "the breath of life [*zoe*]" so that he may become "a *living* soul" (Gen. 2:7) — a *psyche* that shares in the uncreated and deathless *zoe-life* of God. "The breath of life" is God's "holy Breath" *(pneuma)* — which we know by the more familiar translation of "the Holy Spirit." So, Jesus says, "That which is born of the Breath is breath" — a powerful image, and one that suggests a union with God that can only be expressed in mystical and poetic terms. "The wind ["Spirit," "Breath"] blows where it wills, and you hear the sound of it, but you do not know whence it comes or whither it goes; *so it is with every one who is born of the Spirit* ["Wind," "Breath"]."

We must ask what this could possibly mean. At the very least, it suggests a mode of life that is "unknown" to the world — that is to say, one that is unknowable, unusual, "on a different frequency," moving to and from something and somewhere that worldly "radars" can't detect. It is a life as independent of the world's ways as the wind is unconfined. If we understand that John is pointing us towards an experience of God that is mystical in practice, which is initiated by committed faith and baptism ("born of water and the Spirit"), and continued in the life and tradition of the community of God's "children," then we should also understand that John's picture of church life is one focused on spiritual development — closer to a model in which disciples are gathered around wise, spiritually advanced elders, rather than what we are accustomed to think of when we think of "churchgoing" in the West. To "be spirit" — that is to say, to live in the Breath of God to such an extent that our "breath" (source of life) is joined everlastingly to his, and that we now live and move and have our being in perfect, essential union with God's own being — is a mystical experience that only those more adept could understand and impart to the "children" within the "family" of disciples.

This passage is also one of the two in which John refers to "the kingdom of God," as we noted earlier, and it gives us an idea of the mystical content he uncovers in that term. As in the Synoptics, the kingdom of God is understood as present in the world, but unknowable to those outside it (see, for example, Mark 4:26-32; Luke 17:20-21). The mystical nature of the kingdom as a way of life that must be practiced, planted in this age with the coming of Jesus, and growing up and extending itself into the next age, is a concept present in Matthew, Mark, and Luke. That the kingdom is not simply identifiable as a "place," or "the church," or a blissful future existence (i.e., "heaven"), or a kingdom like those hierarchical and militaristic empires the world calls "kingdoms," or anything other than mystical union with God, is likewise gleaned from Paul's description of it, in which he uses the abstract language of *qualities*: "For the kingdom of God is . . . righteousness [or "justice"] and peace and joy in the Holy Spirit" (Rom. 14:17). Notice that Paul in this latter verse says nothing about structure, hierarchy, rules, or any other attribute of an established external organization being the meaning of "God's kingdom." Rather, he describes character as transformed by God's Breath.

When John refers to the kingdom of God, he means the same. When Jesus says to Nicodemus that one must be "born anew/from above" if he is to "*see* the kingdom of God," and "born of water and the Spirit" if he is to "*enter* the kingdom of God," he is using language describing something that must be experienced if it is to be appreciated. "Seeing" and "entering" are things one *does*; they are not things one merely thinks and speaks about in abstract terms. For that matter, neither is *birth* just a metaphor for something speculative. John is referring to an event of new awakening and emergence, one that involves effort, pain, and joy.

This "effort, pain, and joy" is, of course, what is indicated by the statement in 16:21 above. Here we note only that "birth" is, as in John 3, the main metaphor, and that what is "born into the world" is a new *anthropos*.

*　　*　　*

The penultimate event in John's Gospel — the one that sets the stage (11:45-57) for the Passion Narrative and the two chapters telling of the resurrection and post-resurrection appearances of Jesus — is the raising of Lazarus in the eleventh chapter. It is the last and greatest of the miraculous "signs" in John's Gospel. It is a lengthy and dramatic account, full of rich detail and subtleties. It is enough for our purposes to mention that it is not merely a miracle story, but is redolent with mystical significance.

We should take note that Jesus raises Lazarus from death in the midst of the latter's life. Lazarus has evidently died young, but Jesus remarks that the illness that killed him "is not unto death; it is for the glory of God, so that the Son of God may be glorified by means of it" (11:4). After he is raised, Lazarus goes through an "unbinding" of his burial clothes and continues with his interrupted life (11:44; 12:1-2).

Lazarus' death is not treated in a cavalier fashion in the narrative, and Jesus is depicted as being deeply moved by it — indeed, it profoundly disturbs and upsets him (11:33-35). Yet Jesus' "sign" of resurrecting Lazarus is not performed in order that Lazarus might simply resume his former existence, because Jesus lamented the death of his friend and merely wanted him back from the grave. Nor does Lazarus return to become outwardly what he was not before. Rather, he is what he formerly was outwardly, but he has been reborn inwardly. Lazarus represents to the readers and hearers of John the power of Jesus to raise us all to *zoe-life* (cf. 5:24-25) in the midst of our earthly lives, here and now. Lazarus is the outward and visible sign of being "born from above," "born anew." He represents the new *anthropos*, scooped up — if you will — from out of the earth (his tomb) and given the "breath of life" (echoes of Gen. 2:7 again). In all outward appearances, Lazarus remains what he was before his awakening "out of sleep" (11:11). What is changed is his inner life. Indeed, what he faces in his resurrected life is what all disciples face in John's Gospel — the "hatred" of the world and the threat of persecution: "When the great crowd of the Jews learned that he was there, they came, not only on account of Jesus but also to see Lazarus, whom he had raised from the dead. So the chief priests planned to put Lazarus also to death" (12:9-10). And what, too, is "the world's" reaction to this remarkable "sign" and to Jesus himself, who is "glorified by means of it" (11:4)? This:

[B]ut some of them went to the Pharisees and told them what Jesus had done. So the chief priests and the Pharisees gathered the council, and said, "What are we to do? For this man performs many signs. If we let him go on thus, every one will believe in him, and the Romans will come and destroy both our holy place and our nation." But one of them, Caiaphas, who was high priest that year, said to them, "You know nothing at all; you do not understand that it is expedient for you that one man should die for the people, and that the whole nation should not perish." He did not say this of his own accord, but being high priest that year he prophesied that Jesus should die for the nation, and not for the nation only, but to gather into one the children of God who are scattered abroad. So from that day on they took counsel how to put him to death. (11:46-53)

The response of the world to zoe-life and its incarnate bringer is to threaten him with death. Dealing death is what the world and its empires have always known, and still know, and what they do over and over again. The "ruler of this world" was, after all, "a murderer" from the beginning. Since the time of Cain, killing has been endemic to human existence and civilization (cf. 1 John 3:12). In this way, as in others, "the sin of the world" continues.

What John will reveal in his "Passion Narrative," however, is that the Word made flesh will allow the world to take him and kill him, and, by means of his death, he will overcome the world and restore the way to the Tree of Life. And with all this fresh in our minds, we must return to our discussion of the meaning of "the Woman" in 16:21.

# FIVE

# THE WOMAN AND THE GARDEN

*The Fall of Man* (1509)

JOHN'S IS THE Gospel that informs us that "a garden" was the site for both Jesus' crucifixion and resurrection. Not many verses before that detail is imparted, we have the scene of a man and a woman standing at the foot of the cross in that garden:

> 19:25. . . . But standing by the cross of Jesus were his mother, and his mother's sister, Mary the wife of Clopas, and Mary Magdalene. 26When Jesus saw his mother, and the disciple whom he loved standing near, he said to his mother, "**Woman**, behold, your son!" 27Then he said to the disciple, "Behold, your mother!" And from that **hour** the disciple took her to his own home. 28After this Jesus, knowing that all was now finished, said (to fulfil the scripture), "I thirst." 29A bowl full of vinegar stood there; so they put a sponge full of the vinegar on hyssop and held it to his mouth. 30When Jesus had received the vinegar, he said, "It is finished"; and he bowed his head and gave up his spirit. . . . 40They took the body of Jesus, and bound it in linen cloths with the spices, as is the burial custom of the Jews. 41Now in the place where he was crucified there was a **garden**, and in the **garden** a new tomb where no one had ever been laid. 42So because of the Jewish day of Preparation, as the tomb was close at hand, they laid Jesus there.

Not only is the garden the place, then, in which Jesus addresses his mother as "Woman," but it is also where both the angels at the tomb and Jesus address Mary Magdalene in the same manner:

> 20:11But Mary stood weeping outside the tomb, and as she wept she stooped to look into the tomb; 12and she saw two angels in white, sitting where the body of Jesus had lain, one at the head and one at the feet. 13They said to her, "**Woman**, why are you weeping?" She said to them, "Because they have taken away my Lord, and I do not know where they have laid him." 14Saying this, she turned round and saw Jesus standing, but she did not know that it was Jesus. 15Jesus said to her, "**Woman**, why are you weeping? Whom do you seek?"

"The Woman" and "the Garden" . . . It is no great conceptual leap to see in this conjunction of symbols an allusion to the first and archetypal Woman (*gyne*) in the Garden of Eden: "And Adam said, 'this now is bone of my bones, and flesh of my flesh; she shall be called woman [*gyne*], because she was taken out of her husband" (Gen. 2:23; LXX). (We can, by the way, assume with a certain amount of confidence that the Septuagint would have been the version that John and his community mostly used.)

Following the account of Adam and Eve's transgression in Genesis 3, God speaks first to the serpent, then to the woman, and finally to Adam in response to what has occurred. The words of God addressed to the first Woman are of greatest relevance to us in this study. To her, he says in judgment: "I will greatly multiply your pains and your groaning; in pain you shall bring forth children" (Gen. 3:17). As we have seen, John 16:21 echoes these very words, spoken to the Woman in Genesis: "When the woman is in travail she has sorrow."

We turn here to yet another feature, peculiar to the Greek version of Genesis, since it will prove to be significant for our interpretation of John's imagery. It is a striking departure from our own translations, based as they are on the Hebrew (Masoretic) text of Genesis. And it is this: a few verses after those that we have already looked at in Genesis 3, we read in the Greek version: "And Adam called the name of his wife "*Life*" [*Zoe*], because she was *the mother of all the living* [in Greek, the *zonton*, meaning "those who possess *zoe*"]" (Gen. 3:21; emphasis mine). This is the Greek name given to the woman we know as "Eve" — "*Zoe*" ("Life") — and the designation of her children — "*zonton*" ("living") — a phrase that should immediately grab our attention.

With that Greek name, "Zoe," we have in fact the very word that John uses to indicate "*eternal* life." With this, we are getting even closer to a fuller understanding of the significance of "the Woman" referred to in 16:21 and of "Woman" as an address. Might we suppose, then, that any time the word *zoe* — meaning for them "eternal life" — appeared in the shared writings of their community's founding apostle, read in the context of liturgy and their assemblies, the hearers would also have heard and recalled *"Zoe," the name given to the first Woman by Adam?* It seems highly unlikely that they would not have done so. The name of the first Woman, humanity's original Birth-giver, would almost certainly have sprung to the minds of attentive disciples each and every time the word *zoe* was heard read from the community's most cherished texts, as indeed it would have been again and again.

Here I need to be clear once again. I am not saying that the women in John (Christ's mother, the Samaritan woman, and Mary Magdalene) are mere symbols for an abstraction, in this case "eternal life." That would mean foisting a sort of ersatz, "systematic" logic onto an idea that is multivalent, subtle, and poetic in nature. Whatever else the Gospel of John is, it is not a systematic treatise, and its logic is the "logic" of metaphor, suggestion, and poetry. What I am saying is that "Woman" in these specific texts is meant to conjure up a multivalent image, one that is, all at once and intertwined, the archetypal first Woman as "mother" and giver of "life" (zoe-life, that is), yet also the single "body" of the community of Christ's followers (the church as corporate entity, the Lord's "Bride" in both Old and New Testaments, who transcends history), and who — by baptism and the Spirit — is the instrument of rebirth, the restorer of God's life to human beings. John is not a systematic theologian, but he is poetically consistent and mystically coherent.

In John, then, we have iconographic reflections in each of the three women Jesus addresses as "Woman." In one place the mother of Jesus is "the Woman," in another it is the Samaritan woman who reflects this image, and in another Mary Magdalene. There is, however, only one archetypal "Woman" towards whom this form of address always points, who stands above and behind them all, but there are three individual flesh-and-blood women who are thus addressed. In each instance, what Jesus says to these women determines the significance of the allusion, and the context of each statement is also relevant.

Let me illustrate what I mean by returning to the texts we cited back in Chapter 3 of this book.

The first, and arguably the most important, person Jesus calls "Woman" is his mother in John 2:1-12. We know the story. Jesus and his disciples attend a wedding at Cana. The wine runs out, and his mother draws his attention to the fact: "They have no wine." His response, literally rendered, is this: "What is between me and you, Woman? My hour has not yet come" (2:4). Apparently she is not put off by Jesus' words to her, and this is best explained by the logic of poetic reasoning and metaphor — she is not "offended" by a term that is inserted into the text for the reader to interpret, not for her to deal with reflectively or emotionally in any literal sense. In the account she responds by addressing the servants: "Whatever he tells you, do" (2:5). If she represents here, as I have indicated, the Christian community, then this would be an eminently appropriate response for her to give — it is the sort of thing the church would and does say to her "children." We know what comes next. Jesus changes a superabundance of water into a superabundance of wine, which is his first "sign," "and his disciples believed in him" (2:11).

Note here, then, two things: the curious statement of Jesus to his mother: "What is there between me and you, Woman?," and his designation of the hour that hasn't yet arrived as "my hour."

We recall that the hour in which "the Woman" gives birth is designated as "her hour" in 16:21. In 2:4 we have, then, two emphases: "my hour," and the question, "What is between me and you?" — in other words, "What do we share in common?" Looking again at 19:26-27, we receive an answer to that question. Following the words addressed by the dying Jesus to his mother and the beloved disciple, John tells us that "from *that hour* the disciple took her to his own home." So, again, we have the address "Woman," and again the mention of an hour, but this time it is "*that* hour." To put the pieces together: in 2:4, it is "*my* hour"; in 16:21, the hour of birth is "*her* hour"; and now, in 19:27, the hour in which "the disciple whom [Jesus] loved" took Jesus' mother — now the disciple's mother too — into his home is "*that* hour." It is, in fact, *the same hour* that is referred to in all three instances; and what is "between" Jesus and his mother — "the woman" — is precisely the "hour" which is both Jesus' "hour" and "her hour." That is to say, it is the hour when the mother gives birth to the new *anthropos*, who in turn is represented by the beloved disciple (the "founder" of the Johannine community, and the exemplary disciple in the Gospel); and this beloved disciple is the first of many "children" who will be gathered about "the lady." And this *shared hour* is indeed, as 16:21 says, an hour of sorrow and travail — and of *new birth*. The "mother of Jesus" is thus the community and the "mother of all the [eternally] living," the *zonton* of the true *Zoe*.

And this should, of course, put us in mind of the significance of "the garden." Christians from the earliest centuries recognized the locale of Christ's death and burial in John as intentionally evocative of Eden. In the garden the crucified

Christ is certainly being revealed to be the true Tree of Life, and the two standing by that Tree are meant to suggest to the reader the first human beings in the Garden of Eden. Genesis 3 is thus recapitulated, but with this striking reversal: this time the pair is not banished, but instead given access to the Tree of Life (*zoe*).

Turning briefly, then, to the other two women whom Jesus addresses as "Woman" in John's Gospel, we note first his words to the woman of Samaria: "Woman, believe me, the hour is coming when neither on this mountain nor in Jerusalem will you worship the Father." He goes on to say that the hour is coming "when the true worshipers will worship the Father in spirit and truth" (cf. John 4:21-24). That is to say, "true worshipers" will gather from all places, Jews and Gentiles both, and share in "spirit and truth" together as one, united community. There will be no division between Jews, Samaritans, Greeks (12:20-22), and the peoples of other nations. To this seemingly lowly Samaritan woman, with whom he has discussed such high matters, Jesus reveals himself, without any obscuration of the fact, to be none other than the long-awaited Messiah (4:25-26). She promptly goes and proclaims this news to the townspeople: "Come, see a man who told me all that I ever did. Can this be the Christ?" (4:29). The Samaritans then come and listen to Jesus' word. "They said to the woman, 'It is no longer because of your words that we believe, for we have heard for ourselves, and we know that this is indeed the Savior *of the world*'" (4:42; emphasis mine).

The Samaritan woman, then, resembles "the lady" of 2 John, with her "children following the truth" (2 John 4). Although she is a Samaritan and outside the people of the Jews, a particularly despised variety of Gentile, she is nevertheless an apt type of that "church" which transcends "in spirit and truth" all such racial and national distinctions, and has its origins in *Zoe*, "the mother of all the living," the first mother of all human beings and peoples.

As an aside, we should note that there is a parallel in John 10, using the analogy of the Shepherd and the sheepfold for Christ and the church. In the monologue of Christ regarding his relationship to his sheep, he tells his hearers that there are "other sheep" (among the Gentiles, presumably) who are not from the people of Israel: "And I have other sheep, that are not of this fold; I must bring them also, and they will heed my voice. So there shall be one flock, one shepherd" (10:16). So, as the Samaritan woman brings her own Samaritan "flock" to Christ, and they recognize him as Messiah and "the Savior of the world," and in this we see the gathering of both Jews and Gentiles into one church, so too we have the promise in John 10 of there being "one flock" gathered under "one shepherd." And, also, just as we have in John three women who are, in fact, reflections of one archetypal Woman, so we have "other sheep" gathered from other folds. A single theme runs through both John 4 and John 10, and that is a theme of racial plurality united in spirit in the church (one flock, one Bride).

Turning lastly to the scene in John 20 with Mary Magdalene, we have an even more striking reminder of Eden. Jesus' tomb, as we have seen, was situated in the garden of the crucifixion. The cross, as noted above, is the true Tree of Life. From it has come *zoe-life*, amply symbolized by the out-pouring of Jesus' spirit (breath), blood, and water (19:30, 34). When Jesus rises from the dead, then, he does so in this same garden — and it is there, *in the garden*, that Mary encounters him and mistakes him for *the gardener*.

"Woman," says Jesus to her, "why are you weeping? Whom do you seek?" (20:15). With these words we have what is in effect a reversal of Genesis 3:9: "And [Adam and his wife] heard the voice of the Lord God walking in the garden in the afternoon; and both Adam and his wife hid themselves from the face of the Lord God in the midst of the trees of the garden" (LXX).

In other words, instead of the Lord God seeking for Adam and his wife, we have Mary Magdalene seeking for the supposedly mislaid or stolen body of Jesus. When she tries to hold on to him, Jesus says to her, "Do not hold me, for I have not yet ascended to the Father; but go to my brethren and say to them, 'I am ascending to my Father and your Father, to my God and your God'" (20:17). Up until this point in John's Gospel, Jesus had referred to the Father as his Father, not "our Father." But, with this statement to Mary, he opens wide the door to a fully restored union with God — his disciples can now share in his own everlasting relationship with his God and Father. God is now and forever "my Father and your Father too, my God and your God too."

The expulsion from the Garden in Genesis 3 is undone in the garden of the cross and tomb, and the gospel message is conveyed through "the Woman" to his community of disciples. We are then told that Mary, just as the Samaritan woman had gone to the townspeople, "went and said to the disciples, 'I have seen the Lord'" (20:18). Once again, we have "the Lady" who gathers together the "children," this time emerging from the garden in which she was first seeking and then walking with the Lord.

*         *         *

Let me sum up all that we have seen so far as succinctly as I can:

(1) "The Woman" in travail in John 16:21 is intended to remind us of: (a) the first woman, called *Zoe* in the Greek

version of the Old Testament, who is the "mother of all the living," and thus the mother of all peoples and the church; and (b) an "icon" of the community of Jesus (the church), and the same as "the Lady" with her "children" in 2 John.

(2) When Jesus calls his mother, the Samaritan woman, and Mary Magdalene "Woman," he is associating them with "the Woman" of 16:21 and all that she symbolizes.

John's "code," as we have seen, is about the identity of Jesus, but also about the identity of the Christian community. His vision of that identity is that the disciples of Jesus constitute a true and awakened humanity. They are "the living" (*zonton*), rescued from the threat of "perishing" (3:16-17). In his Gospel he symbolically takes his readers back to the Garden and — there — he ushers them directly to the cross and empty tomb of Christ. He wants them to see themselves as partakers of the fruit of the Tree of Life (who is Christ), and enjoying the union with God that was once forfeited in a garden.

John intends that his community be joined to Jesus and the eternal life he gives. This in turn means that his disciples come to know Christ through the mysteries recorded in his Gospel, and to know the Father through Christ, seeing God's glory paradoxically revealed on the cross, and the gift of new life emerging from the garden-tomb. It means, for each disciple, knowing oneself to be among those "children" of God, like the beloved disciple himself; gathered into an everlasting community, which has mystically existed from the beginning, which is also their spiritual "mother," wed to the Lord and therefore a "Lady," and a "sister" among many "sisters."

John's Gospel, unlike the other three, has little to offer in the way of moral instruction. Unlike Matthew, it has nothing to say about communal organization. Unlike Luke in the book of Acts, it has no tale to tell of the practical history and growth of the church. It does, however, give a deep and poetic interpretation of the mystical dimensions of Jesus' identity and ours in relation to him.

# SIX

# OUR PRESENT AND FUTURE LIFE

The Woman Clothed with the Sun,
and the Seven-Headed Dragon (1497-1498)

THE CLASSICAL WAY of reading the Bible is not "literalist" — at least, not in the sense that that term is often used today. As already noted in the first chapter, the idea that a book like John's Gospel should be rigorously historical in its every detail would not have been an aim of its author or editors, nor an expectation of its discerning readers. Historiography as we conceive it was still centuries in the future. This is not to say that historical events were not important at all; quite the opposite, they were regarded as filled with significance and symbol, and thus history was in need of interpretation. In some respects, events of history and outstanding personages were considered to be of even more importance as moral metaphor and portent than they are for us today as mere data. So it was that a skillful chronicler was expected to draw out the significance of events and persons with creative license. This is the point Origen was making about the Gospels' composition, as we saw in Chapter 1 above, when he used the analogy that they were an "interweaving" of history and spiritually symbolic creative license.

For the ancients, to read "literally" a text meant something different than what we usually mean by "literalism" today. It meant the careful scrutiny of a composition itself, its language and what it related on the "surface" level, so to speak. So it was that there was a "literal" reading of, say,

Homer's *Odyssey*, with no intelligent reader understanding that to mean that that poetic epic was a work of history. A text might well contain historical fact, or even just a meager shred of it, but the story it recounted was obviously meant to reflect much more than simple events. The Gospels, therefore, contain much historical detail, but their "spiritual" meaning is drawn out by the Evangelists' skill. Indeed, this is what makes them "gospels" — with the *message* being of paramount importance in them — and not mere biographies.

The Fathers of the church (like Paul, John, and the other authors of the New Testament) read the sacred texts in both their "literal" and "spiritual" senses. The latter, they believed, was contained and conveyed within the former, as the meat of a nut was contained within its shell. A nut needs to be shelled if it is to be eaten, and the literal sense of a text needed to be penetrated and "cracked open" so that the spiritual sense might be tasted. When we read the Gospels (or any ancient text, for that matter), we should bear this in mind: the literal sense contains and exists for the sake of the deeper meaning. Paul is referring to this sort of hidden spiritual meaning contained within the "gospel" he proclaims (though here he is not referring to a written text) when he writes that "our gospel is veiled," only to be revealed to the believing hearer as a shining light "in our hearts" (2 Cor. 4:3, 6).

And the Fathers took this a bit further by breaking the spiritual sense down into three subcategories. These subsets are the *allegorical*, the *moral*, and the *anagogical* senses. (This was so much a commonplace way to read texts that as late as the fourteenth century Dante intentionally implemented it in his *Divine Comedy*, which cannot be fully appreciated without knowledge of these four levels of interpretation — the literal and the three spiritual senses.)

When we read the sacred texts, then, we always have the literal and the three spiritual senses (or two or more of the latter) present. The *allegorical* sense is largely what this book has been about so far. So it was that we saw that "the Woman" in John 16:21 has echoes of Eve (*Zoe*) and is typified in the narrative by the mother of Jesus, the Samaritan woman, and Mary Magdalene; and, as an image put forth in the literal text, she represents allegorically the living church. "The garden" in John is not just a description of the location in which Jesus dies and is buried and subsequently resurrects; it is allegorically the Garden of Eden and thus, by extension, the obvious place for humanity's renewed creation. Allegory points us from the literal text to a reference implied by the latter — a "something else" or "something more" hidden just beyond it.

Having looked at both the literal and allegorical in this book, in this chapter I turn briefly to the other two spiritual senses, the moral and the anagogical. The *moral* sense refers to our ethical conduct in the immediate here and now as disciples of Christ, and the *anagogical* sense refers to our ultimate "goal" or "aim" in Christ — what we are becoming and where we are headed as our transcendent destination. Needless to say, these two senses are directly related to one another — how we live our lives *now* (the moral dimension) has direct bearing on our progress towards our *ultimate aim* (the anagogical dimension).

We have already seen above how "the Woman" in John has an allegorical aspect. But there are both the moral and anagogical senses for us still to search out, and both of these, as it turns out, are (as they were for the original readers of John) crucial for us today. If we are Christ's disciples, then we take the apostolic guidelines for our moral conduct and the vision of our transcendent destination with the same utmost seriousness as our ancestors in the faith did (even though we, as did they, can also expect to stumble and fall short again and again along the way). These two senses are also so closely linked in John that it is impossible to tease the moral dimension from the anagogical. For John, as elsewhere in the New Testament and in Christian thought in general, these two aspects require one another. Authentic Christianity has never overlooked the necessity of spiritual growth and transformation as a prerequisite for final beatitude. We are called to live a new, even rigorous and conscientious, mode of life; and when we fail, we are supposed to get back up and press on. We have a destination to strain towards, and we have a "narrow way" to travel to get there, as every writer included in the New Testament canon testifies.

The moral and anagogical aspects of John are most explicit in his Epistles. The foundation of Christian morality was already laid down in his Gospel in succinct terms: "He who has my commandments and keeps them, he it is who loves me. . . . If a man loves me, he will keep my word. . . . He who does not love me does not keep my words" (John 14:21, 23, 24). In the Gospel, then, Jesus makes it amply clear that obedience to his teachings constitutes *union* (through "love") with him and his Father: if one keeps his words, Jesus says, "my Father will love him, and we will come to him and make our home with him" (John 14:23). "Belief" or "faith" is not distinguished here from "obedience" to the moral demands of Christ: "He who *believes* in the Son has eternal life; but he who does not *obey* the Son shall not see life, but the wrath of God rests upon him" (John 3:36).

A deep ethical line is thus drawn in the sand, and we must choose one side of it to stand or the other. There can be no moral compromise or straddling of that line. If one is "justified by faith" in John's doctrine, it is only with the meaning that "faith" is an ongoing commitment to obedience as the principal evidence of love for the Son. One either keeps Christ's commandments (with the probability of falling short on occasion; see my comments below about confession of sin and restoration in 1 John 2), or one is — despite all appearances or protestations to the contrary — not yet a follower of Christ as one ought to be. This is not a matter of "works righteousness" contrasted with "righteousness through faith alone." Such a dichotomy simply does not exist for John. For him, the issue is primarily "love" made visible in "obedience" to Jesus' words. That, for John, is what is meant by "faith."

1 John fleshes this out more fully and explicitly. The basis of our love for God is his love for us, which precedes and evokes ours:

> 4:8He who does not love does not know God; for God is love. 9In this the love of God was made manifest among us, that God sent his only Son into the world, so that we might live through him. 10In this is love, not that we loved God but that he loved us and sent his Son to be the expiation for our sins. [Compare Paul in Rom. 5:8.]

The basis, then, of our love for Christ is God's love for us, perfectly revealed in the expiation of our sins by the Son. If the church is a community of disciples whose "icon" is "the

Woman" or "the Lady" — "the Bride" of "the Bridegroom" (John 3:29) — then we should mark that this is an icon depicting a relationship of solemn love. We can say with justification that Johannine ecclesiology is, among other things, "spousal" or "nuptial" in nature.

This same spiritual recognition is expressed in the Pauline Epistle to the Ephesians, so much so that the union of male and female in marriage is elevated in Christian thought to the level of an earthly symbol (a sacramental mystery and an image) of an eschatological union: "This mystery is a profound one, and I am saying that it refers to Christ and the church" (Eph. 4:32). And on the outskirts of Johannine literature, in the book of Revelation, we find this image arrayed in full apocalyptic splendor: "'Let us rejoice and exult and give him the glory, for the marriage of the Lamb has come, and his Bride has made herself ready; it was granted her to be clothed with fine linen, bright and pure' — for the fine linen is the righteous deeds of the saints. . . . The Spirit and the Bride say, 'Come' . . ." (Rev. 19:7-8; 22:17).

The anagogical basis for our moral striving is nowhere more evident in John's writings, however, than in the following lengthy and — in part — unsettling passage in 1 John:

> 2:28And now, little children, abide in him, so that when he appears we may have confidence and not shrink from him

in shame at his coming. ²⁹If you know that he is righteous, you may be sure that every one who does right is born of him.

³:¹See what love the Father has given us, that we should be called children of God; and so we are. The reason why the world does not know us is that it did not know him. ²Beloved, we are God's children now; it does not yet appear what we shall be, but we know that when he appears we shall be like him, for [or "because"] we shall see him as he is. ³And every one who thus hopes in him purifies himself as he is pure.

And here is where it becomes unsettling:

³:⁴Every one who commits sin is guilty of lawlessness; sin is lawlessness. ⁵You know that he appeared to take away sins, and in him there is no sin. ⁶No one who abides in him sins; no one who sins has either seen him or known him. ⁷Little children, let no one deceive you. He who does right is righteous, as he is righteous. ⁸He who commits sin is of the devil; for the devil has sinned from the beginning. The reason the Son of God appeared was to destroy the works of the devil. ⁹No one born of God commits sin; for God's nature [literally, "seed"] abides in him, and he cannot sin

because he is born of God. [10]By this it may be seen who are the children of God, and who are the children of the devil: whoever does not do right is not of God, nor he who does not love his brother.

As we can see in 2:28 above, the *present life* of the disciple is to be characterized by "abiding" or "continuing" (*menein*) in Christ and his word — language we first find in the Gospel (cf. John 6:56; 8:31; 15:4-11). Above all, this is a moral statement about the union of Christ with his followers. The one who loves him, as Jesus says, "keeps" his "word," as we saw above; and it is this loving obedience that is here referred to as "abiding." Here we see explicitly that keeping or not keeping Christ's commandments means the difference between having "confidence" (*parresian*) or "shame" (*aischunthomen* = literally, "to shrink away from") "at his coming" (*parousia*). And, in 2:29, we see again the now familiar idea of the disciple as one "born" (or reborn) as a new *anthropos*. And again the description of the reborn human being (i.e., the Christian believer) is presented in moral terms, as the "one who does right" or "righteousness" or "justice" (*dikaiosunen*). This present, passing life of discipleship here is directly related to one's future life in eternity. Morality, that is to say, cannot be relegated to a secondary concern for the follower of Christ.

It is 3:4-10, as noted above, that may cost us a measure of disquiet. Here we see a sharp distinction between the "children of God" and the "children of the devil." The latter are those who live according to the ways and morality of "the world" (cf. 1 John 2:15-17). We can have no doubt that, for John, the Christian is recognized *precisely as one who does not think or behave as the world does*. The Christian, by definition, is one who scrupulously abstains from participating in evil. The moral dimensions of the disorder of "the world" are named in broad terms as "the lust of the flesh and the lust of the eyes and the pride of life" in 2:16. Indeed, the disciple's life is one that comes more and more to reflect the life of Christ himself: "Little children, let no one deceive you. He who does right is righteous, as he is righteous" (3:7). The goal in this life is to so abide in Christ through love and obedience to his commandments that one becomes "sinless" as Christ is sinless (3:4-6). Above all, one must learn to live in the light of Jesus' word; not to do so is to be "lawless," which is what John understands by "sin" (a word that literally means to be "off course").

This would be a despair-inducing passage if it were not for two mitigating caveats. The first is quite simply this: John is referring to a life of *growth* in Christ; growth that does not happen overnight, but requires commitment to development. And this first caveat is underscored, secondly, by the fact that he has previously told his readers that Christian disciples, in their struggles to live righteously, will fail and so will need to confess, pick themselves back up, and keep on moving forward:

> 1:5This is the message we have heard from him and proclaim to you, that God is light and in him is no darkness at all. 6If we say we have fellowship with him while we walk in darkness, we lie and do not live according to the truth; 7but if we walk in the light, as he is in the light, we have fellowship with one another, and the blood of Jesus his Son cleanses us from all sin. 8If we say we have no sin, we deceive ourselves, and the truth is not in us. 9If we confess our sins, he is faithful and just, and will forgive our sins and cleanse us from all unrighteousness. 10If we say we have not sinned, we make him a liar, and his word is not in us.

There is something of a paradox in these verses, of course. If we wish to "walk in the light [= to be "sinless"], as he is in the light," then we must be willing to recognize our sins *as sins*, confess them, and be cleansed from them by the sacrifice ("blood") of Christ. In this way, we return to the path of obedience and love. In time, John presumably believed, the earnest follower would gradually become habituated to a (near-) sinless way of living. For John, the Christian life is a journey through purgatory towards paradise.

And this brings us back to 3:1-3, cited above. Because believers have the hope of being "like him" when he (Christ) "appears" to them, and this "*because* we shall see him as he is," we are charged to be careful to "purify" ourselves "as he is pure." This may, indeed, include the earlier directive to "confess our sins" whenever we have call to do so; but the call to personal moral "purification" is mandatory, and on it rests our "hope." Again, our eschatological anticipation motivates our behavior in the present — anagogy propels our morality.

For John, this is the chief characteristic of Christian community. He can commend "the Lady" because "some" of her "children" are "following the truth, just as we have been commanded by the Father" (2 John 4). This union with Christ and the Father in love is reflected by the oft-repeated expectation in the Johannine literature that Christians should "love one another": "And this is love, that we follow his commandments; this is the commandment, as you have heard from the beginning, that you follow love" (2 John 6). "Love," again, is what lies behind the image of the beloved, espoused "Lady" who, in union with her Lord, begets a family of mutually loving "children." And thus the moral and anagogical senses are based in the idea of union, an "abiding" in Christ through love — love manifested in a good life lived in a radically different fashion than that of the straying world.

★     ★     ★

If we want to see how this icon of the church — "the Woman" or "Lady" and her children — has persisted, developed, and been adapted to peoples in every corner of the world, we can see it, still living and inspiring, in the perennial iconography of the Blessed Virgin Mary. I have already looked cursorily at this in Chapter 2, but in light of what we have just looked at above, it may be a fitting conclusion to recognize how this Johannine (and, for that matter, Lucan) theme has never slipped from the church's awareness. It is hidden, we might say, in plain sight. What is reflected in Christian devotion to Mary is an image of the church herself. She has proven to be the preeminent model of the church as virgin, bride, and mother.

In point of fact, it is those extra-biblical themes, motifs, and doctrines, which became part of the church's tradition from very early on and were incorporated in the church's apocryphal and patristic writings and its art, that most display the mythopoeic themes of John (as well as Luke, Paul, and Revelation) when we look more closely at them.

We can see something of the Johannine emphasis on self-purification, for instance, in the doctrine of Mary's sinlessness, a belief held dogmatically in both the Eastern and Western churches throughout the ages. Its most extreme expression came in 1854 in the Roman Catholic Church, with the papal definition of the "Immaculate Conception." In the East, it simply has meant that Mary never committed sin and kept herself pure — an assertion not only made about her, but also about John the Baptist and others.

Whatever one thinks of such doctrinal developments in general, or of the theme of Mary's sinlessness in particular, the latter is nonetheless congruent with her iconic role as "the Lady" whose children are exhorted in these words to pursue purification: "No one born of God commits sin; for God's nature [literally, 'seed'] abides in him, and he cannot sin because he is born of God" (1 John 3:9). As the exemplar of the church in her eschatological fullness, Mary is rightly typified as "pure" (cf. Rev. 19:7-8; Eph. 5:27, 31-32). This makes good iconographic sense, which the spiritually attuned Christian in devotion almost instinctively takes in. Visualized in the literal image of the Virgin Mother we have allegory, morality, and anagogy all present in a devotionally satisfying mode. This is what John did in his Gospel, and it is what traditional Marian piety has continued to do in a different way. And at an emotional and subliminal level deeper than a straightforward exhortation might reach, both influence the disciple to seek greater purity in his or her own life. In the First Epistle of John the meaning is direct and applied to the receptive mind; in Marian devotion the meaning is received indirectly, perhaps unconsciously, but it communicates just as surely a message of purity and grace. Both have their effect.

Looking at another traditional Marian belief that developed over time, though at a slower rate than the conviction that she was without sin, we can find the theme of "exchange" that has always been fundamental to an understanding of what was accomplished for us in Christ. "He became what we are so that we might become what he is" is a phrase that has been expressed, one way or another, within orthodox Christianity throughout the ages.

In the Incarnation, God the Son assumed our full humanity so that we might "become divine by grace." On the cross, Christ "took away" the sins of the human race, so that we might be united to God's eternal life. By his resurrection the power of death was broken and we have the promise of resurrection in union with him. And one mythopoeic image of this doctrine of "exchange" is to be discovered in the comparison of two traditional iconographic depictions. Forming what is in effect a visual diptych, we have representations (on the one hand) of the Virgin Mother bearing her infant Son in her arms, and (on the other hand) we have the icon of what is called in the West the "Assumption" (the "taking up" into heaven) of Mary. In the icon of the Nativity, Jesus is depicted as newborn, swaddled and tiny; in the icon of the Assumption, Mary is similarly depicted as swaddled and tiny, held in the arms of her Son as a newborn infant. As Christ came into this ephemeral place, this earth, this ebb and flow of time by his "assumption" of human nature from the Virgin Mother, so — in the iconography of Christian devotion — he is shown taking her up from her funeral bier into his everlasting glory. He "assumes" her into heaven. As he "came down" to us through her, so he "takes her up" to himself — and in this we see an image of the church and her "children" in the resurrection at the end of the age.

The Assumption of Mary is an image of the church's victory over death through Christ. An older name, the one used in the East, for this solemn memorial is the "Dormition" (the "falling asleep") of the Virgin, and, as the earliest sources make clear, it was originally a commemoration of her death. But it was also a *celebration* because it was an image of her final triumph, uplifted into glory by the power of her risen Son. The fabulous story of the event, fleshed out and embroidered in the sixth century, tells of her death and of the miraculous conveying of the Apostles from the ends of the earth to be at her bier. Subsequently, according to the popular tale, upon opening her tomb it was discovered that her resurrected body had been assumed and rejoined to her soul in heaven. The early sacred art of the Dormition is particularly touching. It is still the common artistic motif in Eastern Christianity today, but it was once the universal motif of the Assumption, just as common in the medieval West as it was in the Byzantine East. Without going into all the icon's details, at the center of it is typically shown the Apostles gathered about the bier of the reposing Virgin. Above this scene is Christ, carrying in his arms towards heaven the small, infant-like Mary, wrapped in white linen bands. These are, as I have already noted, both burial clothes and a reminiscence of the swaddling clothes in which Mary had once wrapped the infant Christ. The iconic motif of Christ with the tiny, babyish soul of his Mother both mirrors and inverts the image of Mary similarly holding the infant Lord. Here, however, she is the "infant," newborn into eternal life. Her very smallness indicates her absolute dependence on Jesus for her Assumption.

This vital feature of her utter dependence on Christ's loving, gentle carrying of her soul upwards into heaven was lost in Western art after the Renaissance. In the latter she often appears to be superhumanly ascending into glory "on her own steam." Nothing so superhuman and goddess-like is to be seen in the traditional icon, however. Instead, there she is tiny, humble, dependent, and fully a creature. Like the psalmist, the image says to us: "I have calmed and quieted my soul, like a child quieted at its mother's breast; like a child that is quieted is my soul" (Ps. 131:2).

Mary "on her own steam" could not have accomplished her own resurrection; she had to be "assumed" by the divine power of Christ. The traditional icon is, in fact, profoundly Johannine; it eloquently and, especially pertinent for us here, notably says visually what Christ says in the Gospel: "Truly, truly, I say to you, the hour is coming, and now is, when the dead will hear the voice of the Son of God, and those who hear will live. . . . I am the resurrection and the life. . . . Let not your hearts be troubled; believe in God, believe also in me. . . . When I go and prepare a place for you, I will come again and will take you to myself, that where I am you may be also" (John 5:25; 11:25; 14:1, 3).

The icon of the Dormition suggests, as well, by its implicit connection of death and rebirth, the sacrament of Baptism. Mary has died, but has been raised and seated in heavenly places with Christ (cf. Col. 3:1-4). The Assumption does not point back to a historical moment at the end of Mary's life, so much as it points ahead *anagogically* to the future when the dead will be raised. Further, it reminds us that, by grace, we are participants now through baptism in all the promises of Christ: "You were buried with him in baptism, in which you were also raised with him through faith in the working of God, who raised him from the dead" (Col. 2:12). As Mary herself was dependent on her "faith in the working of God," so we, too, are dependent on the same faith. The church, for which Mary is the image, does nothing "on her own steam": "Apart from me you can do nothing" (John 15:5).

Lastly, this provides something for us to take to heart as we consider our own individual deaths. We cannot conceive in any way remotely close to reality what eternal life will be like. After all, what really or conceptually can the text mean, that tells us "we shall be like him [Christ], for we shall see him as he is" (1 John 3:2)? Can we even begin to guess what "being like Christ" implies? The anagogical aspect of our faith remains something wholly beyond our intellect's grasp, and so we must "see" it in the church's matrix of symbols and images. The Assumption and, in Western art, also the image of the "Coronation" of Mary, point to the hope of eternal life to which all Christians aspire. The latter, which is usually represented by a heavenly scene with Mary in the center receiving a crown on her head from an anthropomorphically rendered Trinity, is the Western symbol of what the Eastern church means when it speaks of "deification" — our goal of "sharing" in "the divine nature" (2 Pet. 1:4). Like the glorified Virgin, we "shall be like him," when "the Lady" (the church) will be united with her "Lord."

But for now we have the moral aspect to consider and abide by: while we remain in this world we must strive to live as Jesus taught us to live, to "keep his commandments." Before everything else in Christian discipleship, we need to focus our attention on the practical aspects of living as Christ enjoins us in the here and now. "All who keep his commandments abide in him, and he in them" (1 John 3:24). Then, giving the only thing we truly possess, we place our lives and deaths in the hands of the risen Lord, trusting him to "assume" us after we have departed this life. And that, as we have suggested, is perhaps best pictured in that oldest "Assumption" icon, of an infant Mary, absolutely trusting and dependent, the image of the church and the trusting human soul, tenderly held in the arms of Christ and carried by him into his glory.

&#42;    &#42;    &#42;

And so, what can we say to all this in conclusion? Only this. Everything we have looked at in these pages must converge within us. The literal, allegorical, moral, and anagogical senses of John must work their way into our minds and hearts and souls. If they are to have meaning for us, we must ruminate on them and let them work a healing in our memory and imagination, inciting our wills to live into our union with Christ. "The Woman," "the Lady," the Blessed Virgin, our own reborn souls, united as one voice, speak to us — her "children" — the same word, and say, "Do whatever he tells you" (John 2:5). Jesus in turn says to us, "You are my friends if you do what I command you" (John 15:14). Our souls drink in that word and allow it to engender love within us; love in turn causes obedience to bloom naturally; and conscious obedience gives way to the fruit of union and spontaneous abiding in the Spirit with the Father and the Son. As Augustine said famously in a sermon on 1 John 4:4-12, if we are growing in such a way as this, we will in time know how to "love, and do what [we] will."

This, of course, is the work of prayer and discipline. It requires our effort, it is a constant growth, a commitment to rise up and persevere whenever we fall, but it is a life lived — even in arid and difficult times — with the certain hope that at any unforeseen moment we can know the presence and reality of the indwelling God. Discipleship involves nothing less than our lifetime, however long or short that may prove to be.

As I said at the very beginning of this short book, Christ is indeed married and has taken a bride. He has a family, and it extends to all the children of "the Woman." It is a union of love, and its end is shared life with him — *eternal life*. It is a moral life and a mystical life, born of divine love itself. And so, purifying our selves "as he is pure," may we come to "be like him" and "see him as he is"; and, finally, may this be true of us all:

> In this is love perfected with us, that we may have confidence for the day of judgment, because as he is so are we in this world. (1 John 4:17)